c

o

p

e

For more information, find CCM at:
http://copingmechanisms.net

THE DOUBLES

A BOOK ON FILM

SCOTT ESPOSITO

For Beth,
who has shown me so many new ways of seeing

TL;DR - 7

TL;DR

Mary Ruefle: "I write because I am a writer, and writing, in the course of my life, *has come to be more natural to me than speaking.***"**

So it has for me. Before I speak I polish, I rub my little pebble of dialogue until its smooth flesh gleams, and then I show it around with as much grace as I can muster. I next see the flaws in this pebble and rub it ever smoother. On and on, these words never quite resolving.

To my mind this is more writing than speaking. It has always been this way, and I attest to you that I am a born writer. But then why am I here with a whole book about film?

Watch me work and I will show you. If Ruefle says a writer comes to find writing more natural than speaking, then I will add that listening comes most natural of all. Great writers are first of all great readers, and reading is nothing other than a concentrated form of listening. It is of a piece with observing, eavesdropping, spectating, voyeuring. They are all the raw material of books.

Now this is where film enters. If I am a writer who loves to listen—a writer who *needs* to listen—then I find film irresistible because it is a conversation that lets me savor the luxury of my silence. The images blaze by, and somehow they are language. They tell me about everything: politics, passion, philosophy, science, hilarity, tragedy, theory, prophesy—all the world and all its people are in film. It seeds the thoughts that I will discover as I write.

I have just spoken the truth, but I have not made it strong enough, for film's images do not only surface in my writing. They bubble up everywhere in my life. They have constructed me, and the world that I live in. To write anything at all these days is to explore this filmic world.

I have always understood this. Even as a child, long before I knew that I preferred to scribble words than utter them, long before I theorized about a global civilization wrought by film, I would sit there soaking up cinema's monologue, feeling the satisfaction of it becoming my fiber, the fiber of everything around me.

So it was for years. And then one night a furious swarm of cinematic thoughts occupied my mind. For an entire week they *would not leave*, I had to write them out. I did, it was a fever, two hours later I had my first bite of this book.

Werner Herzog: "Cinema has made a stronger impression upon us than any other form of imagery ever invented."

Exactly what you would expect to hear from a man who has invested his life into film, but who can deny it? I won't. I will stand alongside Robert Sklar, who asks, "are we not all members or offspring of that first rising generation of movie-made children whose critical, emotional, and cognitive experiences did in fact occur in movie theaters?"

Sklar continues, "American culture, for us, may be movie culture." I think it is. I will admit that television might also stake this claim, for it was far more pervasive throughout my childhood than cinema. With luck I would see a few movies in a week, versus hours and hours of television every single day. But TV was a box in our living room, whereas cinema careened all over me, carrying with it so much more of the human world. After all, how much could be said for that little box, which almost entirely excised sex from its rendition of human life, which censored the most interesting parts of the human body, which blushed before strong words and complex language? This little box restrained itself to 22- or 44-minute arcs that were jammed with irrelevant advertising. It showed me cardboard people on cardboard sets speaking cardboard sentiments. And worst of all, its little screen was under *my control.*

But going to the movies was a flight from all distractions, a relinquishment of my life, a place where anything might happen. The heroes of my era shone enormously before my eyes. I saw our common myths. Even the Dolby sound check made me shiver!

William Carlos Williams: "No ideas but in things."

I have always appreciated this quote for its minimalism, severity, and impossibility. No writer can ever reach this most alluring goal. Our ideas will *always* overflow the things that should contain them. The literary form can do nothing but.

But Williams is correct. Ideas outside of things quickly grow abstract, they become tiresome. Any good literary language bristles with beckoning images, it is always ready to offer the readerly mind a branch of thought to alight upon. Imageless ideas should be limited, so why not aim for zero? This will distill your language to a breathtaking imagistic purity, it will turn philosophy to poetry.

But if a writer can never perfectly follow Williams's advice, an auteur will find it impossible to defy. At the movies there are no ideas unattached to things, for cinema is compelled to communicate by showing. Yes, sometimes directors have filmed words on paper, and sometimes a voice-over intones a person's thoughts. Actors even occasionally read philosophy and poetry to us. These things have long happened, and they have always been blemishes on the purity of the cinematic image. Film is most successful—most itself—when its ideas exist in things, unbothered by unnecessary and unwanted words.

And so here is the catch: I adore the purity of film, but I am a writer. I must have ideas outside of things. It is in my blood. And, to be honest, I enjoy a little philosophy. I want to explain what I find in films, to show you how they have lived with me, to give voice to their implicit theories, to transform their visual texture into precise words. I love doing this. But there's always that little voice insisting I should leave these cinematic ideas bound up in their images. I should let them be.

Hitchcock: "Cinema is the greatest mass medium there is in the world and the most powerful."

As I just observed about Herzog, is anybody surprised to hear such a claim from a proud auteur? Isn't it just a little bit dubious, coming from one who had invested so much into film? But just stop to think: what kind of a man was Hitchcock? Do you think he was the sort to settle for second best? If he really believed there were a more powerful medium for shaking the bones of his audience, don't you think he would have found that one and mastered *it* instead?

Stanley Cavell: "The uncanny is [the] normal experience of film."

It is, and I would add that any language is uncanny. Just travel to a foreign nation and observe people speaking words you cannot understand, and you will begin to see how uncanny our means of communication are.

It took decades for film to evolve the grammar beneath its complex articulations, and now each of us must receive hundreds of hours of on-the-fly training in modern cinematic language before we can follow even the lightest contemporary fare. As with the acquisition of our native language, this all happens as a matter of course before we are old enough to even remember that it occurred. Thus does film's uncanny expression of reality become ours, just as these alien and arbitrary mother tongues become our very selves.

Tarkovsky: "Not one of the old and 'respectable' arts has such a mass audience as cinema."

Tarkovsky is indisputably right that film has a much greater mass audience than the great artistic forms descended to us from the Middle Ages, so then why those scare quotes around the "respectable" arts?

Doesn't this betray an inferiority complex, the great practitioner of a still-young form a little too eager to knock some prestige from the elder arts? This inferiority surely relates in part to that much greater audience Tarkovsky claims for film—a clear advantage of cinema over those "respectable" arts, but a mixed one that admits film's uncouth populism.

We should put the shoe on the other foot: if film's mass audience will make an auteur defensive, many a writer will envy that audience. Literature is not a mass medium. Writers must count on being, in Shelley's phrase, "the unacknowledged legislators of the world." Our relevance, if at all, arrives through murky back-channels of influence. (What fortune to briefly become the toy of a celebrity.)

It would be such a grand thing for my modest book to compel one million viewers in its first weekend, a rather sluggish turnout for a major movie. But of course no writer would ever have such outlandish expectations, not even the author of the steamrolling, conglomerated bestseller, which has done a nigh impossible thing if it comes by so much as 100,000 readers in a full year.

Hitchcock: "If you've designed a picture correctly, in terms of its emotional impact, the Japanese audience should scream at the same time as the Indian audience."

No doubt this was one of the reasons Hitchcock found cinema so powerful. As a writer, I burn with jealousy for this power. It doesn't matter if *Psycho* is translated into Japanese, it doesn't even really matter if you pay attention to the dialogue in English, when Janet Leigh gets stabbed you snap into your fetal. Everybody understands this language. What writer wouldn't want such immediacy, such universalism?

But to turn it all around, where is the ripe ambiguity, where is the coy and lingering mystery, where is the aphoristic contemplation in leading a thousand moviegoers to salivate when the bell is rung? As cinematic language becomes more and more broadly comprehensible, it does so at the cost of all those things that a language achieves at its most highly articulate moments.

Serge Daney: "Cinema isn't a technique of displaying images, it's an *art of showing*, and showing is a gesture, a gesture that demands looking."

You can write about a beautiful person undressing, or you can show a beautiful person undressing—which one will better force the attention?

Moving images demand to be looked at, particularly when they are gigantic and suspended off the ground. They draw the eye, they compel identification with the actors, they transmit emotions and desires.

Literature cannot do this. Its response to this visual immediacy is the power of thick description and sustained reflection. A minority preference, to be sure (we live in an imagistic culture), but one that cannot be dismissed. The auteur depends on the talent of the actor to disrobe more singularly than any other person in the history of film, but in the end the power of visual stereotype will be hard to overcome. Whereas with the written word there is so much more freedom to write about a person undressing in a way it has never been written before, and to connect it to ideas that nobody has ever imagined might pertain.

Krzysztof Kieslowski: "We get up in the morning, we go to work or we don't go to work. We go to sleep. We make love. We hate. We watch films. We talk to our friends, to our families. We experience our children's problems or the problems of our children's friends. And the films are there somewhere, too. They also stay somewhere within us. They become part of our own lives, of our own inner selves. They stay with us just as much as all those things which really happened. I don't think they're any different from real events, apart from the fact that they're invented. But that doesn't matter. They stay with us."

Film's inventions stay with us in a way that literature's do not. Literature's effect comes more subversively. It is the slow rewiring of a brain. We routinely read a book for a dozen or more hours, and this long interaction gradually penetrates to the corners of our mind. Our thoughts become altered, and we emerge from books changed people. Whereas film assaults us in 90-minute bursts, like an incident that stabs our memories.

Literature versus film, the slow drip that seeps throughout identity versus the decisive moment that brands the mind.

Stanley Cavell: "We involve movies in us. They become further fragments of what happens to me, further cards in the shuffle of my memory."

When I first read these words of Cavell's I knew it was the germ of this book. I would write about movies that had become cards in the shuffle of memory. It felt right because I knew it had always been this way for me. All my life the cinema was always right there guiding me.

What exactly do I mean? Once in adolescence I was to give a speech. What a terrible speech-maker I was! Shy and soft, clumsy with my articulations, never any conviction in my voice. I knew my fate was to slop it up, but then came an inspiration. I had seen *Pulp Fiction* earlier that year, and I owned its soundtrack. On the disk was a recording of Samuel L. Jackson reciting from the bible, Ezekiel 25:17, a motif of the film. At many points throughout *Pulp Fiction* Jackson had hefted his silver 9mm, towered over his panic-stricken prey, and recited these words with consummate righteous fury. An orator! (His charismatic voice is a thing I can still summon to mind at the slightest temptation.) So I played the track of Jackson's oration, and I spoke these words behind him. Poor work. I sounded in little squeaks and murmurs. I played it again, and again I recited. A little better. Again and again; again and again; at the end of a night I could recite this verse as though it were I who had performed in Tarantino's film. And then next day I summoned Jackson's confidence, his clarity, his ownership of spoken language, I made my speech. My audience could not believe it was really I who stood before them. Was it?

Ingmar Bergman: "No art passes our conscience in the way film does, and goes directly to our feelings, deep down into the dark rooms of the soul."

I find cinema's penetrating power so seductive: its immediate images strike down to my subconscious. This is film's unique gift. If music is the most euphoric art, literature the most contemplative, and painting the most prophetic, then film is the most psychological. It crashes through the bottom of the soul and forces a reckoning with those long-hidden things.

Pessoa: "The worst vice of all is to do what everybody else does."

Spoken like a true writer, or even worse, a steadfast poet of experimental aesthetics. Given the source, a huge grain of salt is advised, although it is certainly possible that Pessoa was most sincere when he wrote this. In his day a prim distance from the crowds was still possible, if only just, and he seems like the quiet, anguishing kind to have preserved that distance.

And as for us? I'm afraid such noble aspirations have long since become taglines of mass marketing campaigns. Don't be like those sheep over there, drink this soda! Of course, many of us still utter Pessoa's words—some even with great conviction—but who really follows them?

The choice to use *vice* is interesting. *Vice* implies inevitability, as though Pessoa already knew that we are bound to join the crowd, it can't be helped. This feels right. When Pessoa wrote these words Europe was being transformed into the greatest mass society in the history of civilization: cities were in rampant expansion, factories churned out consumer goods to stock the mushrooming middle classes. Cinemas were booming, heaping entertainment upon the urban hordes. So maybe he knew that we all were already a part of the crowd, like it or not.

I am a writer. I aspire to literature. That is, I am constitutionally opposed to the vice of doing as everybody does. As I said before, only the deluded still believe that literature is a mass medium. To reject the crowds is practically a prerequisite to spending one's time in crafting lengthy works of words. So yes, I completely agree with Pessoa, crowds be damned—and still I am subject to this vice. Just look: my admiration of film is so great as to be grist for an entire book.

Film claims my identity. It makes me greedy. I want to give my prose what only it can possess. I want its blessings, but I also want to keep my prudent distance from its crowds. Now there's a tension. To accept the gifts and pleasures of this vice, but not be swallowed up by it. To absolve a little of mass society's taint. In other words, the common predicament of we moderns.

1996, THE MYSTERY (PART I)
A Brief History of Time, Errol Morris (1991)

In my mind's eye I see broken, blinking glass strewn across a checkered floor, now shattering in reverse, now a long-necked wineglass rising out of the camera frame.

This memory formed in late adolescence as I watched Errol Morris's tour through the birth and death of being.

Morris used the wineglass to put flesh on the second law of thermodynamics. The universe prefers chaos. Its natural state is disorder, so the glass shatters and scatters. The slivers should not pull together. That defies the history of the universe, which is the movement from order to disorder.

This is time. Being started at a moment of absolute order. It will stop when chaos rules utterly. Time is the expression of this passage.

Our memories strain at this tide of entropy. Our living flesh is a little seam of scheme in a universe always moving toward chaos. Our resilience can only last so long. Eventually we succumb to disorder, we disease, we die, we are scattered atoms.

Aside from that wineglass, Morris's *Brief History of Time* left me with very few conscious memories. I did not, for instance, have any recollection of its opening riddle, articulated by a machine voicing words pried from Stephen Hawking's brain.

Hawking wants to communicate his views on the chicken and the egg. Which came first? he asks. What existed before all existence? As the genius's mechanical voicebox asks these questions, Morris projects the head of a confused chicken before a field of stars. This deadpan literalism is a trademark, a way to trim down the weighty truths his subjects often utter. There are a lot of them in this particular film. *A Brief History of Time* brims with the grandiose: entropy, singularities, time, the birth and death of the universe—they require images to drag them into the everyday. So Morris's chicken gives my eyes a place to focus while Hawking ponders how a human brain could ever imagine what existed before all of existence.

Hawking asks: Will time ever come to an end?

I surely hope it will. As long as I can remember I have always been terrified at the thought of being trapped forever in time. Just imagine if there were no end to this consciousness. No escape. Stuck with one's mind forever. I will always prefer the oblivion of nonexistence to immortality. It is a great relief that one day my sense of self will be erased.

Borges: "Our destiny . . . is not frightful by being unreal; it is frightful because it is irreversible and iron-clad."

Hawking next asks: Where does the difference between the past and the future come from? Why do we remember the past, but not the future?

Past and future. They are so basic that it takes a genius to point out that they are arbitrary.

Morris cuts from the starry sky to tight closeups of the single, enormous button clutched in Hawking's left hand, his sole means of communicating the contents of his brain. His eyes stare into lists of words flashing by on his computer monitor, his face frozen in the expression of a man craning to whisper in your ear.

Now Hawking's mother recounting his infancy. She says that during the blitz, when not a single light burned in all of London, she watched her baby stare up into the magnified heavens, so plain his sense of wonder.

This is where it all starts, is it not? Wonder was the reason I watched Errol Morris tell Hawking's life that night in the 11th grade. I knew wonder existed in the science of the stars.

Those adolescent days I made my first glimpses of the mystery.

The war over, Hawking's childhood. Morris labors to produce freighted memories of the boy genius, but his family has little to share. He liked complex board games, he climbed through high windows. Ho hum. Only in the Oxford years begin the traces of the man the world would know. He's a truant, a lazy student; and still he solves more math in hours than all his classmates in a weekend. His discarded scratch paper is better than their top efforts.

I have always suspected people who claim to know their nature from too young an age. I was certainly never one of them. Until my eighteenth birthday I thought my destiny lay in the institute of technology a few miles from my childhood home. I would play tennis there in the summers. One night I saw Hawking lecture in this place. The sounds of his computer's voice echoed off the auditorium's walls.

I chose not to attend that institute of technology. I traveled hundreds of miles to the north and began to study law.

As I studied there, I veered toward the arts. This took years. Only in my 22nd summer on Earth did I think I might like to be a writer.

It's in the Oxford years that Hawking's body begins to betray him.

You can already see the frame Morris is constructing: as the genius's mind turns opulent, his body turns desolate. Immeasurable mind, immeasurable disease. A one-in-a-billion chance atop a one-in-a-billion chance, pulling in the exact opposite directions.

One of Hawking's friends relates a story from the Oxford years: the genius loses his balance and falls down a flight of stairs. They lay him down, and when they manage to wake him up, he asks: Who am I?

You're Steve Hawking they say.

He has no idea who that is.

How could a mind cease to know what it is? And how could it rediscover itself? It sometimes amazes me to think that we all wake up each morning knowing just who we were the night before. We trust in the illusion that we are those same people who fell unconscious. But we are not. The brain digests the day while we sleep. Our neurons are put right, our whole self is cleaned and tidied; we return, now knowing where we left the keys, the dilemma's clear solution, those few more words for our story. Every night all humanity slides a little toward some different self, but we feel as though we are just who we have always been.

Attracted by Einstein's Theory of Relativity, Hawking begins to study the science of the heavens. He is enraptured by this grand idea that no human being had ever spoken of before Einstein.

And Hawking says, I think I can do better.

At 21 he is diagnosed with a rare early onset form of motor neuron disease. The doctor tells his mother there is nothing to be done. He has two years to live.

As she re-tells this story to Morris, it's plain how incredulous she still is. Anyone can see. For decades now she's told the story of the doctor who instructed her to wait for her son to die. Who literally said, there's nothing anyone can do, just wait for him to die. And this very pleasant, very refined woman is still seething at him.

Hawking says that right around then he dreamed he was to be executed. He knew he was going to die. When he came to he was filled with determination.

I wanted to understand how the universe began, says Hawking.

The Vedas: "Where did this creation come from? . . . Perhaps it formed itself, or perhaps it did not—the one who looks down on it, in the highest heaven, only he knows—or perhaps he does not know."

In 1964, when the genius is 22 years old, he watches

Roger Penrose give us black holes. Penrose wrote the equations that explained what happened when stars died. Suddenly human beings could speak of black holes.

Hawking took this math, and with it he gave us the origin of the universe. What he did was to reverse the direction of time. Instead of looking at matter collapsing into a singularity, he imagined a singularity exploding into matter.

And there it is. We live inside the largest possible explosion. All of reality is the explosion of that singularity, still happening some 14 billion years later.

Hawking was 26 when he gave us the origin of being. How different our world would be if he had never unraveled it for us. And how different *my life* would be if Errol Morris had never asked him to explain how he unraveled it for us.

This discovery was not enough for Hawking. It was not nearly enough. What 26-year-old goes home after his most radical victory? He next wanted to know how that singularity got there to begin with, a thing his very own math said we can never know.

Kierkegaard: "The thinker without the paradox is like the lover without passion."

I understand the lure of a question that admits no answer. A question that stares at you and sternly whispers, *go away*. Such mysteries are my ultimate seduction. A child, I once filled my shelves with books of monsters and aliens. Older, I collected astronomical curiosities. Older yet, I'm still so charmed by any beckoning mystery.

I think I must have inherited this from my father. What else could have led him to spend his life looking at the sky? I once asked if he believed in God, and his answer was the stars. He completed his doctorate in the physics of the heavens just as Hawking was finishing his, and this knowledge brought him to Southern California to guide spacecraft. This is why I was born where I was born. I arrived just as *Voyager* readied its approach to Jupiter.

The photos *Voyager* sent back beguiled me. My father would bring them home on sheets of glossy paper, which then bore the fingerprints of my small hands. He took me out into the night and taught me to stare into the heavens, and I still remember the shock as I brought into my vision four little dots arrayed around the disc of Jupiter. Quasars, neutron stars, black holes, the things physics couldn't answer—what better obsession for a boy? In them I first felt the chill of existential panic. I read a book that followed a single particle through the life of the universe, and it showed me the possibility of infinite time.

It was with these questions that I nurtured the mystery.

One night at seventeen years old I went to see the genius in person. Months later, I watched him in our TV screen, I on the floor, my mother and father on the couch behind me. At that point I was blind to Morris's efforts to humanize the genius, his fascination with what it means to have the most abnormal of brains trapped inside of the most abnormal of bodies. I only understood science. I remember telling a classmate we should put all our money into science, take it all entirely from the arts. And now, when I watch this movie, I notice Hawking's particular way of phrasing things, the unique way he uses the English language, and I wonder: if he had phrased it differently, if he had used different words to interpret his math to the world, would it be a different universe we live in now?

I do not know what my parents made of Morris's film, nor what they remember of it today. I don't believe we ever spoke of it. I imagine their pleasure in sharing something that so clearly pleased me. I was an odd, quiet child who kept his secrets. I felt suspicious of them, I did not know how I could reveal myself. They must have felt me felt slipping away. I picture my parents watching me watch that movie, looking over my shoulder.

In the years since that night, I have always remembered that wineglass un-shattering from the checkered floor. I could always see it in my mind's eye. It is a memory my parents gave to me. A way back to a period that now feels so different from my life.

Hawking's discovery of the beginning of time behind him, his body continued to deteriorate as he pondered harder questions. Writing became difficult, and so he began to develop mathematical equations he could operate strictly inside of his skull. Equations that would take dozens of pages to work out— he did them mentally. It was as if Mozart had composed an entire symphony in his head, said one colleague.

These were his very own tools for researching the universe. Nobody was on his level. He was the only one in the world to understand his tools, the only one to wield them, so they gave him unique insight into the nature of reality.

This is not so different from writers. That's the whole idea behind literary style. To try and construct one's own unique approach to language in order to find a perspective on reality that nobody else has.

Right about the time Hawking was making his mathematical tools, he would be seen ascending the stairs of his home by dragging himself up by the arms.

In 1974 he shared his impossible discovery that particles escaped from black holes.

A colleague stood up in the middle of the lecture and exclaimed that this was madness.

Morris tracked this man down, and there, 20 years later, with a sheepish look he says he later told Hawking he was right.

The genius continued: this same process makes black holes evaporate. More: as a black hole deteriorates, the process speeds up, until at last the rift in spacetime explodes in a blaze.

John Berger: "Everything he has seen contributes to his sense of the enigma of life: for this enigma he finds partial answers—each story he tells is one—yet each answer, each story, uncovers another question, and so he is continually failing and this failure maintains his curiosity."

Hawking wanted to know if this meant that information lost inside a black hole might be reclaimed. Whether what falls in is erased from being, or if nothing is ever really erased.

What a very strange thing it would be for information to be taken from the universe. You could erase your past. Imagine, you have a shameful secret that you never want anyone to know. You tell it to the black hole, and, *poof*, it ceases to exist. In that instant, your very brain matter, and the brain of anyone who might have known your secret, changes.

Morris implies that Hawking chose to study black holes because of his fascination with entropy: whether the flow of time ever turns around. Whether the universe lets our young selves be reclaimed, or if we're strictly prohibited from touching the past. A proper obsession for a man given a death sentence at 21.

I have learned that memories are a little like an old book that's increasingly filled with falsehoods as you read its sentences. Science now says that whenever we access a memory we are physically changing its fiber. The result is that cherished memories become less precise with time, not more. With each recollection they are less the actual experience and more our impression of it. I cannot disagree.

Jorge Guillermo Borges: "I think that if I recall something, for example, if today I look back on this morning, then I get an image of what I saw this morning. But if tonight, I'm thinking back on this morning, then I'm really recalling not the first image, but the first image in memory. So that every time I recall something, I'm not recalling it really, I'm recalling the last time I recalled it. So that really I have no memories whatever, I have no images whatever, about my childhood, about my youth."

In 1981 Hawking saw the Pope. The great Pole told him that the Church found his research acceptable. However, continued the Pope, he should not look into the moment of creation, which was for God, and God only.

With a hint of satisfaction Hawking explains that

immediately before meeting the Pope he delivered a lecture arguing against creation: the universe is self-contained, neither beginning nor ending.

No beginning, no ending, no creation, no destruction. No God.

We do not yet know if Hawking is correct. Physics has not decided whether all being has need of a Creator. But even were it to demonstrate no beginning to our reality, no end, I cannot imagine people ceasing with the Divine. A mere creator and destroyer is a beggared God—what of meaning, morality, justice? Humanity will never reckon with these without a Deity. Physics cannot answer them.

Science stands opposite mystery, it wants answers that do not allow further mysteries. This is what separates it from art, where the strongest answers do not solve the mystery but deepen it.

Hawking is not an artist, he is a scientist, his science has made him an author of our reality. We use his metaphors to discuss the workings of existence. In this he has followed Roger Penrose, who invented black holes, and John A. Wheeler who coined the name. They are authors, too. Those who find the seams in our perception will rename our world.

And you know who else is an author? Borges! Borges is an author! He gave a continent its language, and he gave me a few beloved metaphors. He may have even improved on Einstein in his own manner.

I know the exact day I first read Borges. It was Monday, October 2, 2000. I know this because a copy of *Labyrinths* was placed into my hands on my 22nd birthday. It was given to me by a woman I had met during the summer, and in that short time she had already shown me many authors that changed the language through which I perceived the world.

Labyrinths was the first inscribed book I was ever given, and I immediately felt a great potential to this object. I carried Borges with me on Monday morning to a bank of concrete steps where I waited for a game theory lecture to begin. It was my final year of college. I started at the beginning, three peregrine names: Tlön, Uqbar, Orbis Tertius. So many paths of memory run through that first reading of Borges. That morning on those concrete steps has left a thick residue. It was my first encounter with a way of thinking that would colonize the mystery that had colonized my mind.

Borges: "I now held in my hands a vast and systematic fragment of the entire history of an unknown planet."

"Tlön" is a story of some 5,600 words, it contains roughly 50,000 bytes of data. The capacity of the human brain is conservatively estimated at 1 petabyte, or 1,000,000,000,000,000 bytes—20 billion times larger. So the size of "Tlön" with regard to my brain is close to that of the head of a pin with regard to the Earth. How could such a tiny thing have changed so much for me?

I hoped to do right by the gift this woman had inscribed to me. I needed to let her know that her instincts had been correct when she took the old man from his shelf in the bookstore.

And if she had been proven wrong? Where would I have ended up by now?

But she was not proven wrong, and I owe it to my encounter with Hawking. Because of him, I immediately grasped Borges's world. Hawking made quantum logic intelligible to me, and Borges made my world intelligible to quantum logic.

Some months later I explained these things to this woman.

There it is, the beginning of my inexorable movement from science toward language. After all of this time I still return to Borges, and I now read "Tlön" as a story about how the future colonizes the past. It tells about an obscure book that radiates out a kind of knowledge, and slowly this knowledge appears in more and more places, until eventually it is ubiquitous, and the world has changed. No one can ever remember a time when this knowledge was not everywhere. "Tlön's" narrator watches as this alien energy changes how he and everybody around him sees their world—he is the only one that seems to realize what is happening—and he knows that in a generation no one will be able to remember that things were ever otherwise. So it is with our lifetimes, where the things that are yet to occur change how we see the things that have already occurred to the point that we cannot recall what really transpired. This, too, is what has happened as I repeatedly watched Morris's *Brief History* to write this essay.

My memory of that shattering wineglass was replaced by a memory of a memory of that shattering wineglass. Every time I thought about it, I fixed some new incarnation of that memory more and more solidly in my mind.

In 1985 Hawking lost the ability to utter words. He began spelling his articulations with an assistant by looking at each individual letter. It is such a slow, laborious way of communicating. It's a little like one of these scientists says in the middle of this movie: if you happened to fall into a black hole you would be able to see things no human had ever known, but it wouldn't matter because you couldn't tell anybody.

Some years later, Hawking was given the computer we see him clicking throughout this movie, which must have sped his speech to what felt like a febrile pace. But still so agonizing. So much to say, and the words only getting out in drips . . .

Around that time Hawking began to study the end of the universe. What would happen when that one most godly of all explosions ceased? If the universe begin to contract, would time flow backwards? Would it become natural that the wineglass un-shatter? Would we all return to our wombs?

This is brilliant. By simply reversing the state of being from an explosion to an implosion, entropy reverses. Disorder, not order, becomes the prized commodity. We lament how our rooms always seem to get tidy, we worry about the cleanliness of our environment. We don't speculate on our death for a lifetime but our birth. Our very memories return to us with the force of the future, and we search in vain for the chance to forget.

This beguiling world will not come to pass. It was shown to Hawking that even if the universe does begin contraction, entropy will still increase, time will still flow forward.

The man who proved Hawking wrong is the exact person you would want to extinguish one of your most cherished beliefs. He is smilingly gaunt, indefatigable cheer in an ugly sweater and gigantic glasses. He tells us that he computes, he discovers that the genius is wrong, he breaks the news. Hawking replies, this cannot be, did you consider such-and-such? The student computes, and again he approaches the genius. Hawking repeats, no, this cannot be, did you think of such-and-such? Again he computes, again Hawking is wrong. More quibbles. More computations. Back and forth for what seems like a year, until at last Hawking admits that time will not reverse course.

This refutation made the student famous.

A decade and a half later he built the most powerful quantum computer in the world.

"It is no good waiting until the universe collapses to return to our youth," says Hawking's robot voice, no inflection, no emotions to betray what dreams were extinguished, what beloved fantasies died when he at last admitted that the world's chaos would not one day resolve into order.

With this fable of the genius and his student, Morris signals our flight from the strict and falsifiable realm of science as we move toward the film's conclusion. Now Roger Penrose speaks enigmatically about the nature of consciousness. Quantum physics suggests that what one does in the future might affect what happened in the past. It's scientifically plausible, he claims, that after you die you might become somebody else, maybe someone who previously lived. Penrose has made a sort of grail from the room quantum physics allows for the soul. In the places our theories say are off-limits he finds consciousness and free will. He implies that the universe would not be so precisely calibrated toward our existence if we weren't here explain it.

Hawking: "What is the point of the universe existing? Is a unified theory so compelling that it brings about its own existence?"

Equations are the most objective language we have for describing what we see. They do not interpret the world. What breathes them with life? What makes these symbols into black holes, relativity, time travel, free will, chaos, eternity?

In 2011 Hawking told the world that philosophy is dead. "Philosophers have not kept up with modern developments in science," he said. "Particularly physics. Scientists have become the bearers of the torch of discovery in our quest for knowledge."

That same year he professed his belief that there is no God and no afterlife. Having spent his maturity contemplating the deepest mysteries of existence, he could no longer see any place for these two religious pillars. "We have this one life to appreciate the grand design of the universe, and for that, I am extremely grateful."

I don't think Borges could have put it better.

In my movement from Hawking to Borges I have exchanged the eschatology of cosmology for the abyss of language. I prefer where I am now because language only ever pushes us toward more language. It is an ever-evolving instrument of human perception, and for me, the most compelling mystery of all is how we perceive.

Hawking's mother: "You have to find out what you can't know before you know you can't. So I don't think the mind should be restricted at all. People must think. People must go on thinking."

The last thing Hawking articulates in this movie is a certain hope that one day physics will discover the full workings of the universe, and that these theories will be made comprehensible to all humans. "Then we shall all be able to take part in the discussion of why it is that we and the universe exist." I cannot fault these aspirations, but we needn't wait. What else does literature do but grind exactly that mystery between its stones?

When I re-watched Errol Morris's film some two decades after my first viewing, I saw that it is not a wineglass but in fact a teacup. Morris uses a shattered teacup to visualize entropy, not a wineglass.

For my second viewing of the movie I did not slip a VHS cassette into a tape player. I accessed it through miles of fiber optic cables that connected my computer to another residing somewhere on the Earth's surface. It was still the same movie, no matter that it was no longer an arrangement of positively and negatively charged atoms on a long strip of plastic, instead now a microscopic array of switches spread over an aluminum disc. The teacup had survived this transition. But the teacup that had been recorded through my eyes and saved in my neural architecture had somehow become a wineglass.

Why a wineglass and not a teacup? A ridiculous answer to an impossible question: because of the wineglass in Borges's "Funes the Memorious."

Funes's memory is perfect. It does not lose *a single thing*, so infinite that Funes keeps time by counting the seconds as they pass. His mind seems boundless, but it is not; Borges writes that "to think is to forget a difference, to generalize, to abstract," and Funes cannot do this. He cannot make abstractions because his memory is fiercer than any other object in the universe. When he sees wine he is unable to comprehend the liquid as "wine." He can only see the fluid in all of its unique particularity: it is the singular result of every individual grape that was crushed to make it, the exact bacteria that fermented it, the trees that were cut for the cask, that atoms of air that aerated it, the photons of sunlight and molecules of water that grew its grapes, the galactic debris that first formed the Earth on which they grew, the singularity out of which it all came.

Funes's perfect memory does not perceive as do humans. If not God, he is godlike. A kind of divinity to which science might aspire.

This creature that Borges invented is one possible expression of Hawking's longed-for theory to explain the entire universe. This is precisely what Funes does: he perfectly maps all of existence by knowing the movement of every particle at every second. He knows everything but understands nothing, for comprehension is human and Funes is a living equation. He does not know the truth, he *is* truth. We are not, for if we already were the truth we wouldn't have to invent it. So a wineglass and not a teacup because that is where the truth lies.

1997, THE VIOLENCE
A Clockwork Orange, Stanley Kubrick (1971)

Once the violence is in you, does it ever leave?

The screen is a 40-foot rampart of red.

It is a red pillar sitting on my face.

Red.

The scientific method informs me that colors can affect my mood. They poke that huge expanse of gray matter that thinks before I even know I've thought. Red is the color of danger, the color of viscera, the color of passion and stupid mistakes. The color of rage. This red that Stanley's pinning me with is priming my brain like a canvas.

Stanley's gonna paint all over us.

From the red of rage to Alex's unblinking right eye, false eyelashes pointing from the bottom like spikes. The camera pulls back on tiptoe: Alex and his droogs in white suspenders, white shirts, white pants, enormous white codpieces, black bowler hats, black combat boots. It's all black and white: the pitchest walls behind them, a milk-clean, large-breasted woman on all fours before them, tits up, she's a table, other such statues kneeling forward like supplicant caryatids, their breasts round, erect, creamy, enormous flames of platinum hair.

It's dim in the milk bar, the bouncers stand firm with their grizzly arms crossed, and everyone's drinking a little something extra: vellocet, synthemesc, drencrom.

This would sharpen you up.

Just as Alex and the droogs are limbering their minds for a little of the old ultraviolence, Stanley is getting us all nice and pliable. It would be too easy to show us a bunch of hooligans beat a man senseless. That's not befitting a storyteller of Stanley's talents. He wants us to reflect on this world where it's the height of chic for teenaged boys to drink drug-laced milk from the bare nipples of porn statues. He wants us to see that sick look in Alex's eye and hear his pompous voice declare what's about to happen. Because violence is just violence, that's it. The movies have given us violence, plenty, plenty of violence. That's been done, friends. Violence is normal. Violence is normalized. But Stanley's not your normal filmmaker.

Physical abuse is bad. But emotional abuse—that's where the money is.

Everything in this movie is either violence or the suspenseful anticipation of violence. This is not the commodified, story-at-11 destruction we've all grown bored with, this is sadism, the eyeball-slicing *Un chien andalou*, retch-making filmmaking that we will *never* get used to.

Even the most cut-rate sadist knows how trite it is to beat a helpless bum unconscious. Not for Alex that amateur stuff. He'll surround the poor man and mock him, he'll stick that smug little snout right in his face and make him scream with impotence. Look how angry these gray whiskers get, his puffed out chest. Pathetic. The droogs laugh and knock out his last dreg of dignity. And still, they're holding out a tiny drop of hope, they're dragging out his humiliation so that he knows *they're* in charge—THEY—sure as the sun will rise in the morning, he. is. done. *Done!* To destroy a man's mind—why now you're owning him! Alex wants this bum's soul. He wants to stamp that permanent bootprint on his brain.

And this is just a warm-up, friends. This is just Alex getting his blood pumping. This is foreplay for the little creep. Stomping a bum's face is how Alex prepares his libido to rape, and good old Stanley's going to give us a front row seat.

Because here's the thing about Alex: he doesn't just get high off of this sick shit—he gets aroused. Alex is a sexual sadist. Why else would he and his droogs walk around wearing gigantic codpieces? Why else would Stanley fill this 45-minute-long rampage with so many hard cocks? They are everywhere: graffiti on the walls, subjects of art, lollipops, noses on masks, handles at the milk bar; Alex even gets grabbed in the crotch by a social worker, and he arguably jerks himself off to Beethoven. Outside of hard-core pornography, there are scarcely so many ready dicks crammed into any 45 minutes of cinema.

And of course Stanley makes sure to give Alex a chance to use his own.

In fact there's so much sadistic violence in *A Clockwork Orange* that Stanley earned himself an X rating. Officially he got it for a little throwaway threesome—Alex and two lovely kittens in high speed so as to carefully blur their cavorting bodies—but I don't really believe that's what did the trick. That scene is the least distressing thing in the entire movie. It's consensual. Everybody is having fun. No one gets their blood spattered on their own face, nobody is raped. Just adolescents succumbing to their urges—what could be more wholesome? No, no, no. That scene was just the justification to drop the hammer on Stanley's shitstorm of a movie.

Because the thing is, this film is disgusting. Purely sick. Only a diseased society would consent to project this on gigantic screens for millions of people to see, to call this debauched masochism entertainment. Everyone in this movie is always shrieking, everyone's eyes are always bulging, nobody occupies any less than five times their space. The acting isn't measured out in tablespoons, it's dumped out the back of a pickup truck. This movie overwhelms your eyes and ears with an operatic deluge of blood and semen and misery.

Now here's sweet little me telling you that this movie represents the defining cinematic experience of the 20th year of my life on Earth. The first time I watched Stanley's ultraviolence I had never seen an X. I had hardly even seen an R. I had no idea what an X might even be. I imagined you could only see an X by crawling into a tawdry theater where the seats were covered in juices. I would never have dared ask to see an X. But there I was, a newly minted freshman, and I had just been instructed to watch this X.

So Alex creams that drifter, now he's screaming in his merry cruiser to rape a woman. Not just any woman, a wife. Not just any wife: the progressive and enlightened spouse of a bleeding heart who writes day and night to save the soul of people like Alex.

This is one of the most horrible scenes I have ever watched on film. It's gratuitous, far too disgusting, very unnecessary. The sort of awfulness that will never leave my mind. It cut me, it left scars. I can pinpoint just what makes it terrible: while the droogs hold down the helpless bleeding heart, while Alex cuts the clothes off his wife, them all flaunting their codpieces and wearing creepy, phallic-nosed masks, Alex is joyfully crooning "Singin' in the Rain." He's just as gleeful as Gene Kelly was in 1952, he's dancing about, flinging his arms wide, basking in the screams and tears. Alex isn't just defiling a married couple, he's defiling all of film culture. One of the iconic scenes of Hollywood glamour, one of cinema's real beauty spots—he's violating it, like it's some gorgeous beach on the French Riviera that just got spammed all over with crude oil. He's searing this moment tattoo-deep into Hollywood's tender flesh. This is what has happened to film in two decades. Just 20 years! That's all it took to get from Gene Kelly's naïve raptures to Alex's drug-addled rape. In 1960 you couldn't even show sex. When Hitchcock so much as posed a post-coital woman in her bra in *Psycho*, everyone thought it was the end of the world. And now look! It's 1971. Alex is crooning "Singin' in the Rain" while he shoves his dick in a nonconsenting woman. Who on Earth is going to watch Gene Kelly prance around when Malcolm McDowell is about do to something unforgettably awful? The droogs have taken over, friends! This is what film is now. This is it! Stanley has won. They gave him his

X and he took it, along with 26.6 million American dollars—only 8 other films got more that year.

Stanley knows a thing or two about all this. Back in 1962 he filmed *Lolita*. In 1962 Nabokov's nymphet was chaste as a virgin. Not a single sex scene, just a few double entendres of the kind you can nowadays see in TV advertising. That was all Stanley could manage in 1962! He even said he regretted making the thing because of the damn censors. But just 9 years later Stanley can rape and murder all he wants. He can have bare naked statues of women with drug-laced milk coming out their tits. He can have Alex beat a woman to death with a sculpture of a gigantic cock. Oh it's over friends, it only took 20 years, and Stanley is letting everyone know the droogs have got it.

And me, what am I? Nineteen-seventy-eight, friends, seven years later. I was born into the world that Stanley wrought. I am a product of the tutelage of the multiplex. Too late now. There I was, watching *Clockwork Orange* 26 years after Stanley gave it to the world, a sweet 19 in a post-droog era.

Michel Foucault: "We are neither in the amphitheater, nor on the stage, but in the panoptic machine, invested by its effects of power, which we bring to ourselves since we are part of its mechanism."

Stanley is such a master. Every single time, this rape scene makes me want to kill. A very, very disturbing thing. Those buttons exist, and Stanley knows how to push them. Every time I see the bulging eyes and cracked brow of the bleeding heart, every time I see this poor woman screaming out her eyeballs, I can't help but identify. I know the bleeding heart wants to kill, if he were free he'd take that little pissant boy and tear him limb from fucking limb. How dare you come into my *god damned* house and have the *punk* temerity to fuck with my *fucking* wife! He would bury Alex in eight feet of sand and fill his eyes with honey and watch the flies make a cassoulet of his helpless peepers. And I would do it too.

But Stanley won't give us that satisfaction. He's not going to right this wrong so easily. He's got much better plans for us. He's going to cram us full of rage like a Thanksgiving turkey. Exposed, naked, gagged, gaping, helpless, and there's Alex leisurely disrobing, sticking his ill snout into the bleeding heart's face, filling this woman with horror. It just goes on and on. There is no conceivable reason to keep us here so long. This is pure degradation.

Stanley knows it takes guts to burn your way into a person's brain.

This film is despicable. It is base, disgusting, and horrifying. Sweet youthful me. I'd never lived away from home, but now I was in a dormitory watching ultraviolence.

I had never seen a thing like it.

And sure as the point of Alex's knife, I liked it.

I did not yet know how easy rage is. I thought rage was hard, it made me feel like a man. What an estimable, mature thing: to feel my rage, to want to kill on behalf of the wronged. So foolish. Rage is not hard. Not hard at all. It is a very, very easy thing.

Stanley made me want to kill, and he gave me images that have stuck for decades, and that's not so easy. He did this all in 10 minutes flat. And every time I watch these 10 minutes, they are just as horrifying and murdersome as they have ever been.

Now here's another side of Stanley's star boy. Alex, you see, isn't any mere thug, he's a thug with a religious adoration of Beethoven. An earnest tinge of awe enters his voice every time he speaks the name "Ludwig van." He hangs a portrait of the composer's face in his bedroom. He buys recordings of all his music and listens to the Ninth Symphony every night. He so venerates the master that he delivers an excruciating smack to his beta droog Dim when the bearish child *pfffts* at a woman singing the Ninth's chorale at the milk bar.

All those liberal pieties about art ennobling the human spirit and making you a better human being—Alex is their wall.

What difference does it make that Europe's very archetype of the romantic genius wrote his Ninth as a paean to brotherhood? What difference at all? Beethoven is what thrusts Alex into a religious ecstasy after a night of beating, robbing, and raping.

Beethoven neatly pegs the social failure that makes *A Clockwork Orange* churn. What to do with the remainder society cannot absorb? A Romantic outcast like Beethoven makes things simple—he naturally aligns his genius with goodness—but Alex sees pleasure in death. So then what will society do with such a member? Will it claim he's a fly in the ointment, or will it grapple with the truth that he, too, is it?

Eminem: "So many lives I touched, so much anger aimed / in no particular direction, just sprays and sprays / and straight through your radio waves, it plays and plays / 'til it stays stuck in your head, for days and days."

A perfect example of what I mean: Alex smacks Dim hard when he insults the master, and Alex pays a price for this. Insubordination is in the air. It's not right to treat Dim like that. The boys are getting a little tired of their king droog's cocky manner. So Alex comes downstairs from his parents' apartment to find the boys speaking rebellion. Things are going to change. You're not our master any longer.

Alex deals with them in his own consummate way. He lets them overplay their hand, he lets the confidence plump them right up. And then he strikes. The leader of this little insurgency goes flying into the river. Dim goes there too. And as the lumbering, shocked, gape-mouthed dolt makes his way to shore, Alex extends a hand in brotherhood, he takes Dim's little paw into his own, and Stanley takes care to show it in very slow motion as Alex delivers Dim a nasty red scar across the top of his right hand.

The look on Dim's face. I'll never know how Stanley could summon such wailing demons.

The insurgency crushed, Alex suggests a little adventure to improve morale: there's a wealthy woman on the edge of town, and they can make a lot of easy money if they rob her. So the droogs cruise to her mansion, they try the old trick. Alex raps on the door and begs her to open up. There's been a terrible accident, miss! My poor old boy is bleeding to death on the road! But this woman is too wise, she's not about to open her front door to this lie. So then Plan B: a second story window left open.

While they do that, the woman grows suspicious. She's read the news about gangs of marauding teenaged boys. She calls the police. They dispatch a car at once.

Clever Stanley. Taking his time to build up the scene, encouraging my mind to imagine the possibilities. Will she escape? Will the cops arrive in time? Will Alex win again? It's this suspense that lets me identify with the victim, this identification that Stanley leverages to make her ultimate fate so damning.

This woman is a bit of an odd cookie. Her home is crammed with cats, and she seems to enjoy parading around in a leotard and tights, contorting impossibly amid her languorous felines, her walls covered with enormous erotic canvases of lesbians. Why she's such a rubber maid, it almost looks as though she could lick herself to pleasure! And as a finishing touch, she's collected a bust of the one and only Ludwig van—sitting right opposite an enormous erect phallus and its two ripe testicles on an elegant wood table.

It's this sculpture that Alex takes immediate notice of when he steals into her room. His wide-eyed goggling is almost sweet: the boy's never seen such décor, and now he can't decide whether to rob her or compliment her good taste. She brings him back to Earth with a tirade, and in turn he smacks her cock on the head. We now discover a strange property of the object: it's weighted down with liquid, so when it's nudged it responds spasmodically, pumping up and down just like a real cock in the throes of sexual energy. As Alex stands there insulting and infuriating this woman, she lashing back with equal vigor, the fake cock pumps up and down. Stanley positions his camera so that Alex is almost entirely blocked by this expressive dick—

and the conclusion is inescapable. This sculpture represents the action behind Alex's zipper that Stanley can't show us. If it weren't already perfectly clear, now there can be no doubt: Alex gets horny off of inflicting pain and humiliation. This little *pas de deux* is his way of getting it up. How could he possibly leave without a nice, hot shag? The cock pumps, the woman berates—and Alex grins. What fun for the little scoundrel! Now this degenerate dance, the woman thrashing at Alex with her bust of Beethoven, he keeping her at bay with his gigantic cock. Head-to-head—head against head!—this increasingly chaotic choreography, until with one last, wild swing the woman falls to the ground, and Alex, standing astride her, raises the cock up high with both arms. He aims that gigantic dick right down at her gaping mouth.

That next instant, one of the most loathsomely violent things I have ever seen upon a screen.

I remember when I first saw this, I was numbed. This is not just a repulsive violation of a woman's body, it is one made with an unmistakable bale energy. There is such deep-bred misogyny in this image: an enraged, helpless woman getting force-fed her own pretentious cock art by a contemptuous adolescent. Alex standing above her, shoving it into her with the full power of his two strong arms. It is utterly vile. Filth. There is a particular violence in stuffing a person's mouth. To make a woman taste what she doesn't want in there, to shove it in against her wishes, to steal her breath, stifle her voice, muffle her humanity.

And then that final image. For two decades I have always remembered exactly how he cuts away at the moment of impact. Instead of showing this phallus cracking the woman's teeth and bloodying her gums, he juxtaposes split-second flashes of her erotic art. Her gaping mouth becoming the gaping mouths of the artwork. In this moment she is a not a human, she is a mannequin.

For the first time in this film Alex looks abashed. He had not intended for this to occur, and he realizes that this is too much.

The cops are coming, he flees, he emerges through the mansion's front door—who is waiting for him but Dim, clutching a bottle of milk in his bandaged right hand. For the moment of betrayal Stanley jumps to a tight shot of Alex in profile, time slowed so that when the bottle impacts his left temple I can luxuriate over the beauty of the shattering glass, the ballooning white liquid. And then ears are filled with Alex's screams. He is curled up in a ball, his droogs running merrily away.

If the first third of Stanley's film is the violence of the citizen, this second third is the violence of the state. It is not simply that the police smack and spit at Alex, the jailer screams at him, the criminal justice system abuses him, the prison chaplain manipulates him—it is that they can do no other. As sociopathic as is Alex, the state exhibits its own sociopathy, and what's more, I'm made to cheer it on. Vengeance is on the table, and I'm now screaming for it. Lock him up! Defile him! Ruin his ugly little mind! Make it so this filth never touches another person!

So that's twice now that Stanley has made me disgusted with what he can find in me.

After two years of prison Alex sticks his ginger hand in the trap jaw of the Ludovico Technique. Modern life has flipped the mayhem switch, the prisons are overflowing with sociopaths. There's not nearly enough money for rehabilitation, and anyway, how could the social workers compete against the totalitarian jailyard? So to hell with it all. If prison can't make evil men love good, then it will make them fear evil.

And it will do it cheaply. Efficiently. All with a bureaucratic order.

The idea is to shoot up Alex with nausea-and-terror-inducing drugs and then brainwash him into feeling that pain whenever he thinks of violence. And how are the doctors going to fill Alex's head with images of violence?

"We're just going to show you some films," says the doctor.

You really have to hand it to Stanley, he sure as hell nailed it with that line. If any doctor ever wanted to try out the Ludovico Technique, he'd have all the horrible images he ever needed in any modest film collection. Stanley knows he's a part of this, he understands the power of the image, its capacity to brainwash us. He knows Alex's smirking face will become a part of that. So this right here, this hilarious little deadpan by the quack doctor, this is Stanley saying, I just Ludovico'd you. I just made you watch an hour of fury, vulgarity, and rape.

But why? Why provoke us and disgust us? Why make a film of unquestionable misogyny? After all, Stanley is a humanist. He made a pacifist's war film, he made the world's best indictment of nuclear weapons, and he made the greatest sci-fi flick of all time, which is also a paean to the nobility of the human spirit. So how could he do this?

A good question. *A Clockwork Orange* does have noble intents. It's an acid satire. It wants to make us better. But the way it chooses to educate is the most despicable method I could imagine. Why must Stanley rub my face in the shit in order to save me from it?

Our discipline becomes us.

The doctors jack Alex full of drugs, they lock him in a straitjacket and force his eyes into metal clamps while they screen the worst horrors cinema has to offer. There's even a nurse dripping water in his unblinking eyes, using a little napkin to soak up the excess from Alex's apple cheeks. I love the detail of that! In the midst of this most incredibly inhumane medical experimentation, there's a nurse ever so careful to dry the errant drops off of Alex's cheeks. A fine little piece of Stanley's black humor!

At the end of Day 1, when Alex has been confronted with the sensation of his own death and force-fed horror for hours—I myself am on the verge of vomiting—the doctor proudly says: "you're becoming healthy." Such black irony, it's right there with *Strangelove's* "Gentlemen! You can't fight here.

This is War Room!" And were the point not yet clear, no sooner has that self-satisfied quack pronounced Alex's health than Stanley jump cuts to Day 2—Leni Riefenstahl. Such health!

But I really have to ask how this is different from what Stanley is doing. Is he not force-feeding me the worst in humanity in order to make me despise it? Is he not revealing the very worst in myself? I admire how Stanley implicates everybody: Alex, the sociopath who is being punished; Ludovico, a freak on par with Mengele; society, which accepts this form of justice; film (including Stanley) which mainstreams depravity; and myself, who observes this torture with fascination. None of us can stand outside this violence.

Joan Copjec: "Instead of an external opposition between the subject and society, we must learn to think their necessary interrelation: the very existence of the subject is simultaneous with society's failure to integrate, to represent it."

I am a creature of this violent world. I am the offspring of a self-contented suburb whose point in life is to Ludovico the next generation of Ludovicos. I was duly Ludovico'd, I was on the exact path to becoming a professional Ludovico who would Ludovico the next generation. And I come from a nice place! All the food you can eat, a top-flight education, green lawns, all-American sports, 300 days of sun per year. The property values are enormous! After 19 years of this I was so well-Ludovico'd that I screamed for Alex's blood.

And it's a good thing I did. If it weren't for Stanley, who would have ever told me that Ludovico had been slicing my brain a million ways all my life?

The prison sequence concludes with theater. Before an audience of wardens, therapists, and preening ministers Alex is brought on stage. First he bootlicks a man who smacks him to the ground. Then dear Alex is shown impotent to even poke his pinkie into a naked beauty. Thunder at the conclusion of each demonstration, bows, and Alex heaves on the ground.

Make no mistake. Alex loves evil every bit as much as ever, he's just castrated. The state cares nothing for Alex's soul. It doesn't want to make him good, it just wants to get him out of the way. The bureaucratic god is not humane, it is efficient. Its justice is not salvation, it is order. Discipline and punishment merely legitimate its power.

Foucault: "The search for truth through judicial torture was certainly a way of obtaining evidence, the most serious of all—the confession of the guilty person; but it was also the battle, and this victory of one adversary over the over, that 'produced' truth according to a ritual."

A last, crucial detail: Alex has been errantly conditioned to feel the nausea of death at Beethoven's Ninth symphony. An interesting inclusion, for this music has the notable reputation of being the music of European brotherhood. In fact, just as Stanley was making his movie, this music was being enshrined as the anthem of a united Europe. And this glorious symphony was the exact thing Stanley chose to embody Alex's particular estrangement from his society. Because of Ludovico, Beethoven's spirit-salving music makes him want to die.

Thus does society solve its leftover. Let him walk among his fellow men, he is marked.

We are now in the clockwork portion of this orange. Cured Alex returns home to his parents' scorn. They now have a boarder, and he's more a son to them than Alex ever was. He limps away in shame. Bereft, suicidal, he wanders the streets and trips against that old bum he once beat so savagely. Recognition, outrage. With a mighty yowl he chases Alex into a senile plague of wrinkled meat. Alex is of course helpless; he can do nothing to fight back. As the indigent men smack and stomp, he fully realizes his position. He's not released from jail at all, he's surrounded by jailers at every turn. Anybody can punish him whenever they want. Alex is the sole resident of a new dystopia where anybody—anybody!—can execute the state's disciplinary violence.

I watched this movie. My first semester at college ended. Then came the springtime. Foucault's *Discipline and Punish*. The medieval spectacle of Damiens the regicide, his delirious execution so different from the secrecy of modern justice. I discovered Benthem's panopticon, the absolutely intoxicating idea that someone had tried to build a jail where the prisoners were perpetually spied. How perverse these thrilling visions, Damiens' legendary torture, this hall of godly surveillance. Hadn't Stanley learned quite a bit from Foucault? As I made my first incursions into the poststructuralists, I took my first steps away from Ludovico and the violence he had put into me.

Who drags Alex from the murderous senile slobber? Why it's the droogs, now employed as police! They've exchanged their codpieces and suspenders for truncheons and bobby helmets, everything else remains the same. Before you can say *up shit creek!* they manacle Alex, they haul him to the edge of town, they hold his helpless head in a tub of fetid water, they laugh as his locked hands shake and his bowels empty, they smack him left and right and leave him shrieking in a vicious rainstorm. Wrecked, exhausted, defeated, broken, his brain is nothing but the animal urge to crawl out of the downpour.

A familiar doorbell. As Alex rings, Stanley shoots our friend the bleeding heart with the exact same shot as last time Alex darkened his doorway. Everything has changed. The furniture is new, he is a ravaged man, his wife is gone, she's replaced with a gigantic manservant. The bleeding heart knows. Every twitch of his face screams the truth despite his calm and hospitable lies. Eyes curled up into pate, fingers clamped on knees, face wriggling, a body so stuffed with rage that it's shattering before us.

Alex is cleaned and dressed and treated to a spaghetti dinner. The bleeding heart and his enormous manservant stare down at him as he consumes the food. HAVE SOME WINE, he screeches at Alex. The boy trembles, he stares at his cup and takes a hesitant sip. It's not poisoned! In relief he drains the glass. HAVE ANOTHER! He has another.

Breaking bread, sharing alcoholic beverages, these things mean conviviality the world over. But the bleeding heart and his manservant are not eating. They are not imbibing. They do not look convivial. How could they at a time like this? When you hear the twisted voice of the scum who raped your wife bellowing "Singin' in the Rain" in your bathtub and instantly feel a rage you've repressed for years. Violence demands its release.

Freud: "Why do our relatives, the animals, not exhibit any such cultural struggles? We do not know. Very probably some of them—the bees, the ants, the termites—strove for thousands of years before they arrived at the State institutions, the distribution of functions and the restrictions on the individual, for which we admire them today."

Alex's wine is cut with sedatives, he awakes in a locked attic, Beethoven's song of brotherhood roaring below. The bleeding heart read about Alex in the papers, and now a cat's grin spreads across his mad face as this most beautiful music becomes ultimate torture. Unbearable agony, Alex breaks a window, one long, long step into the sky———

His entire body encased in plaster, a hospital ward all to himself, the public outraged over the sweet young man disfigured with a dehumanizing punishment. The ruling party must reclaim him as a symbol.

What chills me about this penultimate scene is where the violence has gone. In walks the minister who Ludovico'd Alex, lackeys all around, Windex smile on his face. Each man tests the other. Alex gapes his maw so that the minister may fork steak into his mouth, and the minister gestures to two enormous speakers ready to play Beethoven's Ninth. You cover my ass, I'll cover yours, we'll both make out just fine.

The horror of this productive stalemate.

As these two men produce empty smiles for a battery of flashbulbs, I know that neither one of them has grown any less base and self-serving than when Alex's unblinking eyeballs were slung into their metal clamps. But now instead of knifing one another they'll perform this managed, mature form of violence. Progress! Alex will no longer rape, his new friend will provide him with as many concubines as his tireless cock can take, he will no longer thieve, the minister will fund him with the taxpayers' money.

Progress of a sort, this hypocritical, state-sanctioned violence.

And also progress: this vile movie that has caused me to reflect.

The last shot: Alex's patched-up mind envisions his rejuvenated self impaling a bare-chested, white-stocking'd blonde.

"I was cured all right."

And that is health! In this world of Ludovicos run amok it is very healthy to push our violence behind the politician's sneer and the cinema's screen.

It still galls me how easy it is for Stanley to push my buttons.

Every *single* time I watch this damn movie.

Rage fills a man with the emptiest pride I can have. Flush with these worthless funds, I have sometimes felt on my face the grotesque distortions Stanley seared onto his actors' mugs. When I can feel that wail upon my mouth, I fear the mirror. And at the same time, I know that right there in that violent expression is some irreducible quantity of humanity, a thing that must remain a part of who I am, though I will never control it, and always despise it.

To be human is to know some necessary violence, to allow any more is to bathe in acid.

2001, TO BECOME A MERMAID

Suzhou River, Lou Ye (2000)

Czesław Miłosz: "I grew up, after all, in an era that was unlike any other; and what made it basically different was the motion picture."

In 1917 the UC Theater in Berkeley, California, began to display the fantasies of humankind. It was not a movie theater, it was a nickelodeon; it only cost five cents to spend time bathed in the stories we were just learning to tell. According to the Bureau of Labor Statistics of the U.S. government, this would amount to a cost of 94 cents today.

The UC opened two years after *Birth of a Nation* wrenched films from being cheap, fixed-perspective, short-duration spectacles to a medium with unique rhythms, telling new tales for a modern humanity. It so continued showing mainstream films for mainstream people until the 1970s, when new ownership began taking it in a decidedly more artistic direction. In 1977 the UC became widely known as the best place to participate in the carnivalesque rite that had begun to surround the *Rocky Horror Picture Show.* In 1978 Werner Herzog ate his shoe there after simmering it in duck fat in the kitchen of Chez Panisse, his way of fêting Errol Morris's first documentary, duly premiered afterwards. As these honors accumulated, it collected a pleasing sheen of glory and became known to the dorks behind the counter at the video rental store as *the* place to see foreign and risky film.

All told, the UC projected our collective dreams for 84 years, until 2001, when it was closed down because no one could afford to safeguard it against the next big earthquake. Of the several Berkeley movie theaters that survived from the era of the nickelodeon until the third millennium, the UC was the only one to never remodel into a multiplex. From birth till death it contained just one screen, some 1,300 seats fanning out around it in three large wedges.

Javier Marías: "In literature, as in life, we don't always know what is part of a story until the story has reached its conclusion."

I knew nothing about the history of the UC Theater when I stepped into it for the second and last time in spring 2001. I was not there to genuflect before a palace of cinematic art. I barely even knew what good film was. I was just on a date. In my right hand I clutched the hand of a woman. For several months we had been two people falling in love.

She says: "If I leave you some day, would you look for me forever?"

He says: "Yes."

She says: "You're lying."

Water is the biggest metaphor. It covers nearly 3/4 of the planet, it's nearly 2/3 of our bodies. It's the well of life, essential to survival, the foundation of the world's storied cities, the veins of any great nation, the boundless expanses we have not yet tamed. It moves perpetually, perpetually formless, always poised to assume any shape, penetrate any crevice.

If we fall into it, it will kill us. Every year thousands end themselves by leaping from the extraordinary bridges girding great cities. The appeal of this death is in its simplicity, poeticism, and symbolism. Oftentimes when I am walking in the hills not far from where I make my home, I can look across the bay and see the Golden Gate Bridge, a landmark that is considered to be the second-most-popular place to commit suicide on Earth.

The first-most-popular is the Nanjing Yangtze River Bridge in Nanjing, China, not all that far from the Suzhou River in Shanghai.

Suzhou River is a movie about suicide by water, about a kind of love that people depend on to give form to the chaos of their lives, about what happens when that story breaks. As I watched it, it became part of my story of falling into love.

The Videographer likes to float down the Suzhou River and record Shanghai with his handheld camcorder. "If you watch it long enough," he says, "the river will show you everything." It will, but only because it happens to flow through the biggest mass of urbanized humanity on Earth: modern-day Shanghai, 24 million people. "There's a century's worth of stories here, and rubbish."

A place like Shanghai demolishes traditional notions of love. When you're looking for a mate, how much choice is 24 million people? This is hard to grasp. Imagine the average American supermarket, 47,000 different products. I go at least once a week and I still lose track of where to find things. Now picture walking down the aisles of the grocery selling 24 million items. You need just 1 product, the one that you are "meant to be with." How would you ever decide?

This is very different from the Middle Ages, when our notions of romantic love were hammered out. Communities were tiny—in the year 1400, a high point population-wise, all of Europe held just 80 million people, scarcely three times the size of Shanghai. Travel was rare. You would probably have been born, grown up, fallen in love, and died all in the same tiny village. On those scales there would be some hope of finding the person you were "meant to be with."

That's not how things are now. The astronomical odds of love in Shanghai, I would argue, is basically the experience of all of us who live in the modernized world. Though our cities aren't quite as enormous as Shanghai, we do travel everywhere, we communicate flawlessly over immense distances. The pool that we are choosing a single mate from is ungraspable. In fact, never, ever has there been more choice. Thus the flood of dating apps, hookups, swipe left, swipe right, the constant pressure to trade up, the oppressive fear of missing out. With so many beautiful, qualified people to choose from, is there any other sensible reaction? It beggars the notion of "right choice." The one person on Earth you are meant to be with, that's ridiculous.

And still, I believe there is necessity in these bonds, because they form the backbones of our narratives. We are all hewing out the stories of our lives, and nothing is more integral to that story that your life's great love. The people that my master narratives depend on stabilize my sense of self, they give me mileposts, a compass, a means of forward motion. Without such people, the story I tell myself about myself would dissolve. As the innumerable details of our lives intersect, I can see a kind of mysticism, an agency beyond comprehension, and that exerts a binding force on who I am.

Anthony Giddens: "Romantic love introduced the idea of a narrative into an individual's life."

And how complex are the paths that bring any two people together in the Chinese mega-city? Director Lou Ye's Shanghai is nonstop hustle. Everything here is constantly buzzing in frenzy—deals, dealers, dealing, delivery, cronies, thievery, vice, dives, bleeding, beating, exes, extortion, kidnapping, suicide. All this turmoil in a gray zone. We never figure out who these people are, where they came from, what they want to become. They are just pure vectors of desire whose paths sometimes cross, run parallel for a while, terminate, fly off in their own directions.

The Videographer is the prototypical hustler. No steady job, his livelihood depends on exposing as many people as possible to his pager number, which he stencils day and night onto any Shanghai wall. "Pay me and I'll shoot anything," he says. "I'll even shoot you pissing or making love." The Videographer has a camera, he's sort of a film guy, but don't mistake him for a purveyor of personal fantasies. He's not that kind of film guy. "Don't complain if you don't like what you see," he says. "Cameras don't lie."

One day he gets a call from a seedy bar that wants to

advertise its mermaids. The only distinguishing thing about this trash heap is that it's got an enormous aquarium front and center. The Happy Tavern's boss wants the Videographer to film his mermaid shimmying through the floodlit water so he can spam it around Shanghai and get all the leery men to have a beer.

Of course, when the Videographer sees Meimei's lithe, bikini'd, blonde wig'd body corkscrewing through the water he falls right in love.

Let me stop right here to address this idea of some middle-aged guy in a crap suit hiring a video hustler to film a woman dressed as a mermaid to advertise his crummy bar. How much sense can this possibly make? It's shoddy plotting, a little ridiculous, and what's more, Lou is blatantly cramming in symbolism by the pound here. This amateurism is a feature, not a bug, for *Suzhou River* is a movie that proudly garbs itself in rags. From front to back it's all duct-taped contrivance, this particular scenario being a perfect expression of Lou's aesthetic, which might be described as "who, me?" meets a handy cam. If it works at all, it's because Lou is such an impulsive, manic filmmaker, he machine guns the story at you, just keeps piling symbol upon character upon image upon plot twist, it's nonstop southpawing. So before I can even begin processing how absurd this premise is, I'm swamped by all these beautiful shots of Meimei swishing through the water and mugging at the Videographer's camera, and then he's calling her pager at a gigantic yellow pay phone, and then they're ambling together down some neon-lit boulevard, falling in love, Meimei's screen presence just soaking up all the energy in the shot.

Hitchcock: "The fact is I practice absurdity quite religiously!"

Suzhou River is such a grimy, slipshod film (I mean this as a compliment!) that I'm tempted to believe Lou's an affiliate member of Dogme95, or at least an enthusiast. Just like those guys, he's always making do with whatever's at hand, and if there happens to be a little lint on the lens (which very distractingly happens in a pivotal scene about 27 minutes in), well leave it there! Lou's generally grouped with China's so-called Sixth Generation, a school of filmmakers famous for shooting on microscopically small budgets, and whose handheld cameras and ambient sound give their work an amateur feel. Probably this willingness to grime around in cinema's trashheap is an asset to Chinese filmmakers like Lou who are forced to work at the margins. The fact is, in Chinese cinema you can't get screened without kneeling at the feet of the censors, so many directors forego that entirely, meaning that their projects will be poorly financed, shot on the sly, and have only underground, illicit distribution in China. *Suzhou River* was banned in Lou's home country for many years, it was seen the world over before it was ever legally seen there, and because Lou had the temerity to make it, the government officially banned him from filming so much as a single scene for two whole years.

Speaking of amateur, I've never seen in any other movie what I see in *Suzhou River*, which are the arms of the Videographer, our first-person protagonist, angling into the frame from either side, as though the camera lens was right in the middle of his head. The effect kind of resembles a point-of-view shooter like *Doom* or *Call of Duty*. This is all we ever see of the Videographer, just his hands and the occasional forearm, no face, no torso, no legs, feet, shoulders, eyes, mouth, hair, none of that. Just these two arms. I'm tempted to think that this all began as some sort of a joke, that Hua Zhongkai, who voiceovers the Videographer, just said to Lou, why don't you hold the camera, and I'll stand behind you and reach around with my arms, and then they tried it just to see what would happen and suddenly realized that it's perfect. Myself, I love the simplicity of it, the—I'm tempted to say elegance—the absolute literalism to the point of naïveté, the way it works in spite of itself, which is the only way it could work. It's campy as fuck, and I think that's the point, this odd gambit trumpeting the permanently makeshift ethos of everything in *Suzhou River*, this in turn reflecting Lou's vision of 24 million souls hashing out life in the 21st-century mega-city *par excellence*.

Wong Kar-wai: "I make films mostly by instinct."

These Instagram-before-Instagram shots of the Videographer and Meimei lol-ing through Shanghai and falling in love are just about perfect. All at once they're elegiac and wistful while also capturing the poetry and electricity of romance. It's just a woman wearing sweat-shop-surplus, blowing cigarette smoke, popping bubbles, underexposed, overexposed, dancing up to a pylon and giving the camera a deep look while a little wind blows through her hair. Do you need anything more? Do you need eight make-up teams and ten-thousand-dollar dresses, perfect lighting, an aching score, or are those just the excesses we've grown accustomed to? Then they're in her bedroom playing pattycake, their hands moving into impossible accelerations, that most remarkable wolf's grin on Meimei's face, and again I have to say that this is all so utterly simple, so—I'm tempted to say elegant—this basic, completely literal gesture that I love for its effortlessness.

Now we're in the Videographer's shabby apartment, broad daylight, a heavy rain, he's watching Meimei try on dresses as she prepares to go out. How he stares. His steadfast eyes. Fixed. She's pulling the fabric up over her head, revealing her skinny body in black lingerie, zipping herself into another dress, primping, pulling on a cool leather jacket and throwing him a big smile as she blows a kiss. The Videographer's voyeurism is the calcium giving *Suzhou River* its shape and strength. Now he's peeping down on her crossing the bridge of the Suzhou River, dwelling in his fears of abandonment, he'll surely lose Meimei one day, pure paranoid mutterings while he spies on just about anyone.

Meimei is the kind of woman that you don't know exactly how or why she's so desirable. If you were to ask me what her best feature is, I couldn't say, nothing really stands out. She's just your everyday girl. If she faded into Shanghai's millions, nobody would notice. And yet Meimei has got remarkable magnetism, she's the kind of woman I don't get tired of seeing move about the screen, that cinematic presence I always want a little more of.

Maybe Meimei knows her life is way more banal than she deserves, maybe when she's mermaiding around her big old fishbowl she broods on the drooling men and decides she deserves something extraordinary, because one day she tells the Videographer he should be more like this guy Mardar. Mardar! Who the hell is Mardar? He's a motorcycle courier who gave his life over to searching for a woman he lost. Meimei saw it in the paper. This woman, she leapt from a bridge and drowned herself in the Suzhou River, but they never proved she died, so now her would-be lover spends day after day searching Shanghai for her.

Which come to think of it is creepy and obsessive and makes out Mardar to be like the Chinese edition of some American named Darko who's wrapped in a black cape and sporting sweet studded boots—and don't people find guys like this compelling because they're just *going for it*, in the way that we're not exactly going for it in our stable little lives feeding ennui with Sartre and $15 cocktails at that trendy bar? Why *wouldn't* Meimei want this? I mean, she's dating the Videographer. And, to be painfully honest, I do picture our workmanlike filmmaker as the kind of tolerably mediocre dude that you're forced to assume must harbor positive qualities, because someone who seems so trite couldn't possibly score a catch like Meimei, or at least couldn't keep her.

Wong Kar-wai: "We are always in a routine. Most of my films deal with people who are stuck in certain routines and habits that don't make them happy. They want to change, but they need something to push them. I think it's mostly love that causes them to break their routines and move on."

Mardar comes screaming into *Suzhou River* on his chopper with a tight little close-up and a jarring sound like a dump truck cramming the accelerator. It's all shrieks and dissonance, a powerful moment, menacing, frightening even, and I've always been struck by how it's completely undercut by the motorcycle helmet Mardar's wearing. It's this childish little bowl-like thing, and even if you put James Dean in this helmet he'd look like an elf. I have no idea how a it reads to a Chinese audience; to my eyes it just looks meek, not dangerous or motorcycle at all. Maybe this is Lou's way of saying that Mardar can't possibly fit the badass persona he seems to want, or maybe he actually thought this helmet enhanced his masculine appeal. I don't know. It's always struck me as odd, I clearly recall thinking this the very first time I saw Mardar all those years back at the UC.

When I stepped into the UC Theater to watch *Suzhou River*, I'd hardly been in any movie theaters outside of the great Southern Californian megamultiplexes, enormous atriums with a vaguely museum-like feel that led to complex arrangements of halls. The aesthetics of those icy amphitheaters were nothing like the art decos in downtown Berkeley, where instead of a gladiatorial arena you would cram into a box-like chamber, almost a chapel. At that point I didn't notice how these changed surroundings subtly but definitely changed the experience of a film. And nor did I think about the context a movie was made in. Like, for instance, the fact that Jia Hongsheng, aka Mardar, was something along the lines of China's Robert Downey, Jr—once a top actor, he fell into drug addiction, and *Suzhou River* was his comeback vehicle. Nor did I know that Zhou Xun, who plays Meimei, is a mega-star, now acknowledged as China's leading actress, this a role that helped propel her to super-stardom. I certainly wouldn't have reflected on how strangely appropriate it was that Jia and Zhou fell in love on the set of *Suzhou River*, remaining in love for four years, until 2005; and I would not have felt the eerie tragedy of the fact that five years after they fell out of love, in 2010, Jia committed suicide by leaping to his death.

All of this is purely second-nature now, this way of looking at all the contextual extras is so deeply embedded I can no longer make contact with the naïve moviegoer I was in 2001. To get back there, I'd have to strive for another 16 years to forget everything I have learned about watching movies over the course of the last 16. This understanding of art has rearranged the architecture of my brain matter, all I have left now of the old me are kernels of memories that are still somehow accessible. I can for instance recall that on my very first visit to the UC they had shown three consecutive previews for each film in Krzysztof Kieslowski's *Blue*, *White*, *Red* trilogy; I retain a strong memory of very cleverly surmising that after *Blue* and *White* we must now be shown a preview for *Red*. This certain memory was a thing I thought back to approximately seven years later, when I actually did watch *Blue*, *White*, *Red*—seven years, the distance between a point of total ignorance, and a point of being able to anticipate, comprehend, and relish Kieslowski.

Seeing *Suzhou River* was one small lesson in this decade-plus refashioning of my cinematic brain. The same has happened with the great love that has dominated my life these 16 years since; I've again and again re-adapted the narrative of this relationship to fit my mind's new dimensions.

Now we get Mardar's story, as told to us by the Videographer, and *Suzhou River* becomes a story-within-a-story. It's very weird how, after Mardar's introduction, the Videographer begins to relate substantial events in his life, despite not knowing anything about all of these intimate details. He very blatantly just starts imagining who Mardar might be. Right when the Videographer's formerly straightforward love story begins to become murky and complex, the movie jumps from the literal truth of the video camera to the very shaky truth of hearsay, imagination, and memory. Certainly this is what happens to all of us would-be lovers as those breezy first weeks of our relationship give way to the negotiated truth of those long-haul affairs.

To represent that we are now in the Videographer's mind—and not his video recorder—*Suzhou River's* camera angle switches from that awkward, *Call of Duty*-esque first-person to a very tight third-person, so tight that it occasionally feels like first-person and I forget that I'm no longer in the point of view of the Videographer. The camera is still as voyeuristic as ever. It's wandering through Mardar's junky apartment in the middle of the night, it's watching him watch himself in the bathroom mirror while he brushes his teeth, even zooming in to get a closer examination.

Mardar is a motorcycle courier, who, among other things, is paid to give rides to a young woman named Moudan, actually the same actress that plays Meimei but looking 10 years younger. She's not wearing sexy dresses and mermaid bikinis; instead she's got on juniors outfits and has her hair pulled to opposite sides in two girlish ponytails. It's not exactly clear if she's merely supposed to look like a child or actually be one, an ambiguity that Lou does just about everything he can to play up.

Moudan conceals a lot of sass beneath her childish reserve, picking little arguments with Mardar about his old-lady-like motorcycling, resting her head on his shoulder, making him take extra-long routes so they can be together longer. It's clear what's happening. In the big falling-in-love scene, Moudan greets Mardar by stretching high up on her tippy toes and flinging her arms akimbo, one hand holding a mermaid doll, the other clutching a bottle of her wealthy father's signature product: buffalo grass vodka. If that's not a metaphor for Moudan's complete ambiguity as a feminine presence in this movie, I don't know what is.

But even though Mardar is clearly growing attached to her, he remains ambiguous, inscrutable. The camera tends to focus in on Moudan, leaving Mardar as just a muscular arm and a thick torso that gestures at her in some lumpy manner. When we do get to see him, his eyes are often hidden beneath the visor of his motorcycle helmet. Even when he and Moudan are alone in his apartment, his head is frequently turned away, his grim mouth forever paused on the journey to an actual semiotic expression, his eyes staring out somewhere far beyond Moudan's face.

The heartbreaking night that Moudan swoops in on Mardar's apartment unexpectedly and tries to force herself on him, he's just as deadpan as ever. Maybe he's not interested, maybe he is. Who knows. On this rainy, pivotal night, as she shows up with tears in her eyes, clutches him, and just cries and cries and begs him to love her, Mardar is as steely and silent as ever. It's a heartbreaker.

Shortly after this reckoning, Mardar and this shady older woman he's kinda, maybe seeing concoct a plan: they're going to kidnap Moudan and ransom her. My gut tells me Mardar doesn't want to do this, he knows Moudan really trusts and loves him; he resists, but he's pretty heavily outmaneuvered, so he gives in. He gets Moudan drunk and takes her off to some abandoned building, sits her down on a piss-stained couch. This scene is so agonizing because it's doubtless that Moudan thinks this is it, they're finally going to have their tryst. She gazes at Mardar with a playfully insolent look and starts kissing him—for a moment maybe he's on the verge of just saying *fuck it all* and giving in— but then that grim between-expressions expression pops back on his face. He shoves her down. And she keeps popping back up and he keeps shoving her back down, a little more forcefully each time, she's looking more and more deflated. Lou keeps the camera right on Moudan's face so that you can see the message getting through shove by shove. I can't stand watching her hope turn to rejection, that rejection turning into the worst kind of betrayal.

As the wait for the money drags on, things turn toxic. At one point Mardar takes Moudan out to pee like a dog, just sits in a corner of the roof and watches her, this ultimate humiliation, this blatant power that says *you are nothing at all to me*. And it's here that Lou takes a tight shot of Mardar's face, for once we can see an expression, the gravity of this dire turn sinking in as he looks out onto the hazy sun ennobling the Suzhou River with a golden hue, the soundtrack welling up, something a little like the opening movement of Sibelius's Second symphony, grandiose music of Western angst.

This is how mermaid legends get started. It's only after you lose something forever that the memory of what you had becomes real enough to destroy you. You need the chance to make it right, but you won't get it, because she's already dead, when the ransom gets paid and you stupidly blurt out that she was worth just $50,000, you know that you did it, you should have said it was $20 million at the least, $50 million, you're priceless, but when you said *I sold your trust for $50,000* you took whatever was remaining in her and burnt it to a crisp, you'd need at least a lifetime to make it up to her, but you're not going to get that, you're just going to get 10 feverous minutes as you chase her surprisingly quick body through the streets of Shanghai, that body popping itself up over the guardrail on a bridge crossing the Suzhou River, that little preening smile filled with revenge, that last dead stare—this stare you'll always remember, it will haunt you—no longer childish, now womanly regret, damning you, this face you loved growing smaller and fainter as it falls down into the water.

Mermaids are of course creatures that are one-half woman, one-half fish. They are among the oldest literary tropes—Ancient Greek coins have been found depicting the goddess Atargatis, whose mythical transformation into a mermaid was told well over a thousand years before Christ. Like many mermaids, Atargatis was a female who made her transformation after leaping to her death following a romantic disaster; her continued existence in mermaid form represents a transitional realm, a living death where once-women are still of this planet, yet are of foglike consistency, occasionally seen but impossible to touch, forever estranged from human society.

I think, too, we can read the mermaids in *Suzhou River* as a commentary on what film makes us into. In the cinema we are all mermaids. We leave the bright and empirical realm of the everyday to descend into a darkened room only tenuously connected to the outside world, and within this realm of illusions we are capable of being absorbed by gulfs of fantasy. Meimei swims the plexiglassed waters of the Happy Tavern; we moviegoers swirl through the emanations of our unglimpsed yearnings, still very human yet also now celestial, still completely alive yet also now in communion with ghosts. We become dual in film. Were we to discover heaven, it would perhaps be akin to these flashing lights, these oceanic spectacles made from the world's untouched thoughts.

Hitchcock: "When cinema was invented, it was initially used to record life, like an extension of photography. It became an art when it moved away from the documentary. It was at this point that it was acknowledged as no longer a means of mirroring life, but a medium by which to intensify it."

Mardar's backstory ends, it's years later, the Videographer has just met Meimei and fallen in love with her, now Mardar has returned to Shanghai after years in exile. The Videographer is still inventing Mardar's story, in fact he even pauses to remind us that he's *really* making it up now, and since Lou's movie is a love story there's only one place it can go: Mardar accidentally discovers Meimei in the Happy Tavern, and he instantly thinks he's seen his dead Moudan come back to life.

Through Meimei's dressing room curtains he spies her transform into a mermaid. For the second time, Lou's voyeuristic camera stares as this beautiful woman dresses, only now it is not the Videographer's point of view but Mardar's, the entire frame blackened except for a vein of action off-center. Mardar peeps as Meimei transforms into a salaryman fantasy, she takes a long blonde wig, a bikini top, a fish bottom, the neon lights of the Happy Tavern splash pink, daisy, and cornflower all over her, this long shot is filled with deep shadows, the whole scene slightly garish and with dream-like edges. Meimei's back is turned, her face is only visible in reflection as she fixes herself in the mirror, then she meanders up, moves about the room, stares off in the private gaze that we reserve for when we feel absolutely alone.

A provocative symmetry is at work: the Videographer first watched Meimei dress to play herself in the dingy streets of Shanghai, Mardar now watches her become an object for a completely artificial environment. This romantic dialectic is the heart of *Suzhou River*—it is also the line we tread when we become moviegoers—this is a film about blending up the mundane and the impossible, the fancies we force onto the objects of our affection, the realities that damn the dreamers. In the aesthetic of *Suzhou River* the mermaid is a powerful memory: the week-long fuck that can never be equaled, the lost love that fills your eyes with distance. So when Mardar watches Meimei transform into the mermaid, it is at once to see Moudan lose her childish ambiguity, to have his stifled feelings for her flame up into absolute passion. Two desires—one at the forefront of Mardar's mind, the other deeply buried in his subconscious—suddenly fulfilled in one lengthy voyeurism, the film's longest take, its most singular visual scene. Mardar will never have anything quite as good again.

The music in this long moment is a strange aural mélange. First it's a Chinese pop song faintly washing up from the bar, then an Eastern-sounding flute playing a lingering, nostalgic melody; next, something resembling an ambient beat asserts control, itself transforming into a guitar'd tango-esque song of longing and passion, and then at last the symphonic Sibelius music begins riffing in and out over the tango. The effect is dislocating and postmodern, the entire film chopped and mixed into a wishful, wistful montage.

How long will a nice girl tolerate being stalked by a creep? Will her heart soften if he tells her that she reminds him of a dead woman he loved? Will it seem to her more creepy still, or will it instead become seductive if he insists she *is* that woman? Will it make a difference if this latter-day, Shanghai-born Don Quixote cuts a far more romantic figure than her current dull bed-body? Will she perhaps begin to wish she was this woman? Will she find ways to convince herself that she might be her? For how long will she prolong her tedious relationship when this passionate fantasy beckons? What will she do when she decides she wants this fantasy? Will she rush off and leave her video-boy behind, or will she give him one last chance to prove himself to her?

Alain Badiou: "In love the individual goes beyond himself, beyond the narcissistic. In sex, you are really in a relationship with yourself via the mediation of the other. The other helps you to discover the reality of pleasure. In love, on the contrary, the mediation of the other is enough in itself."

Clearly, Mardar spells trouble for the Videographer. The more this good-looking, intense bro with the great eyes comes and tells lovesick stories to Meimei, the more he insinuates in her a dissatisfaction that grows and grows until, at last—a pretty ugly fight—and then, dénouement: if it's not exactly a break-up, it's pretty definitely a break. But just when it looks like things are finally going Mardar's way, somebody hires a thug squadron to beat the living shit out of him as he's exiting the Happy Tavern. This kind of makes him crack. The first thing he does after putting his face back together is pop on over to the Videographer's house and tell him that he's heading away to look for Moudan—at last he's acting like Moudan and Meimei are two different people. He also tells the Videographer that Meimei really loves him and implies that they belong together.

What the hell has just happened? Is getting beat to within an inch of your life the *Suzhou River* equivalent of electro-shock therapy? Why is Mardar suddenly talking sense? And why does he decide to confide in his romantic rival? I don't get this turn of events at all, and nor do I particularly grasp why the Happy Tavern is suddenly closed down the next day. Within the space of about 5 minutes everything in this movie has gone back to zero. The Videographer is alone, the bar that promised to change his life is gone, Meimei is nowhere to be found, Mardar has left, Moudan is no more. It's just as though this story were never told.

I'd argue that this is a consummately cinematic plotline, the business that shakes up the narrator's life but then suddenly disappears, ultimately feeling no more real than a dream. It's a standard of noir, a powerful cinematic genre that's peerless for evoking the absurdity and isolation of modern life. I also find utterly filmic how this sort of plot pretzels itself and unapologetically comes to naught. Film has this privilege that we deny to the other arts. Films can be insubstantial, they can be daydreams. They don't need to have a deeper meaning. They're to pass a couple hours in a comfortable chair in a climate-controlled room, a thing you do with a woman because you and she need a thing to do in order to be together for the night. Movies are not like books or paintings or symphonies, where the investment is so much greater and where the experience is fused to an apparatus meant to usher you toward respect, gravity, profundity. Movies can just be a couple of restful hours. That was my first experience of *Suzhou River*—imagistic, rapid, confusing, a gauzy bright make believe. I didn't exactly get it. I mixed up the characters and found it more a feeling than a story. Who cares? I was sitting next to this woman who I was going to spend the whole weekend with, this was our way of making it start. So that was what that night became in my memory, a cinematic romance projected onto my own personal romance, a little like the ache of nostalgia preconceived, some presentiment that one day I'd eye this memory with longing. As if looking at the deep blue spring dusk sky over Berkeley as we walked back from the UC I purposely thought I terribly wanted to touch that blue, so that I could fix that sensation of wanting to touch the blue in my memory forever.

I sort of wish I'd just left *Suzhou River* as that lovely, foggy memory of a perfect early night in a romance that would grow to my life's all-encompassing love. We watched it once again, she and I, several years later when DVDs were ubiquitous and you could get any one of 100,000 movies delivered right to your home. For years this movie lived in us like a ghost, but now it was much too simple to track it down again, it was a cheat to so easily retrieve what belonged strictly to that night. Enough then, or maybe even too much. But then this film project came along, and I began to feel very strongly that *Suzhou River* was a part of it, so now I've gone and watched it maybe a dozen times and know every little thing there is to know and so have plastered over that space in my brain. If I try really hard I can still get a little sensation of that date, the trail that winds through the Cal campus, the dark blue of dusk, she and I very much in that moment and not wanting anything else.

But of course you know this isn't the end.

The Videographer gets a package: a note from Mardar and a bottle of buffalo grass vodka. Blankly roaming Shanghai, Mardar just happened to find Moudan working as a clerk in a 24-hour convenience store. He walked in, she asked him what he wanted, he requested a bottle of buffalo grass vodka, and when he realized who she was she finally looked adult. At last they're together, but not for long. Police summon the Videographer to the banks of the Suzhou River, where he finds two dead bodies. So intoxicated, they didn't ever want to touch reality again.

The Videographer tells Meimei, they spend all night together like old times. One last, perfect night, and then in the morning Meimei can't resist asking the Videographer if he'd go looking for her too. Of course he says he would, and she just looks down into her hands, her head shaking no. "You're lying," she says, "things like that only happen in love stories." He caresses her hair one last time, the next day he hops over to her houseboat and finds a short letter waiting for him.

She's right. He doesn't look. He gets drunk on vodka. "The best damn drink I ever had," he says. "Nothing lasts forever."

There you have it, a perfectly prosaic individual, left behind by one who reaches toward a fantasy. And why not—can the perfectly prosaic really be in love? Should a woman who wants true love accept a man who doesn't care for anything more than just reality?

There's a reason why movies are the most ubiquitous date, love needs fantasies, it needs love stories, without those it crashes against the unimpeachable facts. Films have always nourished she and I. Our third date, Hitchcock's *39 Steps*, we began to swim within the images of our collective dreams. An uncountable number of dates later, let's call it one-hundred-and-one, Lou's unreality became another story we shared. And now, as I recount those days, we are still here in love, still looking, still doubled in images, still in possession of each other's memories, imagination, these forms as multiple as the water.

2003, ART'S FADING SWAY

Russian Ark, Alexander Sokurov (2002)

I have often fallen asleep in small theaters. It is an embarrassing thing to have happen during one-man shows, and I am certain that at least one actor, a man whose work I have enjoyed on many occasions and whom I admire, saw me sleeping during his. I dropped off right in the middle for about 15 minutes, third row of ten, center seat, and for the rest of the time I felt the reverse of what I should have felt: I felt *him* gazing at *me*. Had he seen? Was he watching to see if I looked bored? If I was going to fall asleep again? It was a small community theater, so right after the performance he was waiting in the lobby to greet everyone. I stepped into that room full of tension, and the person I had came with prolonged my distress by asking to linger and look at the displays for upcoming shows. All I could do was stand across from him and feel his presence pushing ever more into mine.

Robert Bresson: "No marriage of theater and cinematography without both being exterminated."

For a long time I thought something like this was beyond the reach of film. Instead of pursuing the kind of heat you can feel in the theater, film had gone a different direction: it had gone montage. Instead of showing what had been recorded, the movies would be made of innumerable takes patched together into an idea of cinematic reality. I cannot overstate what a happy decision this was for film. Film was never meant to be just theater recorded for posterity: it had to develop its own way to communicate. Understanding the laws of montage meant that, as an art, film could finally be itself. It could now tell its own stories.

No longer was it a faddish technological spectacle destined to fade from the public's imagination. It could compete with novels to be the preferred middle-class entertainment.

But in gaining montage film gave up the heat of spectacle. Henceforth film would be fussed over to the very last inch. Such familiarity breeds cliché. Directors would have to work to get their players to give uniquely energetic, cinematic performances. The very best films would fight to exceed the medium's limitations, and the most average would huddle in its safety. Watch enough of these latter films, and you'll see the same phrases and tics repeated ad nauseum, how they give each film a genetic resemblance. You will see how they strive to give the audience what it wants, which is to repeat the things that they have previously paid to see.

Walter Benjamin: "The alignment of reality with the masses and of the masses with reality is a process of immeasurable importance for both thinking and perception."

When I first watched *Russian Ark*, I was a young filmgoer who tended to watch banal films. I had managed to see a few good movies that had left a deep impression on me, but for the most part I had poor taste. I was drawn to this movie by its singular conceit—I knew enough about film to recognize what a radical idea it was based on, and I was immediately intrigued. This was a point in my life when I was beginning to become fascinated by the weird forms that auteurs sometimes attempted to impose upon their movies in a quest for originality.

I pulled it down from the video rental store shelf and took it home. For the next hour and a half I spaced out. I didn't get it at all. But I always remembered that night, this movie stayed with me, it was something I knew I would have to return to when the time was right.

So what is this singular conceit behind *Russian Ark*? Well, perhaps the best-known and most daring way to break from film's sameness is to shoot long takes. This requires a great deal more forethought on the director's part. It limits the ability to edit, and it makes it much more likely that some lifelike mistake will slip into a shot. The long take is such a potent force for innovation, in fact, that if someone wanted to be all-but-assured of making a unique movie, they could do something without precedent: make a 96-minute film composed of just one shot. This would be a little mad, since they'd be depriving themselves of the chance to edit the film, a little like asking a novelist to write a book all in one nightmare-long session. They would also be exposing themselves to the risk that some garish blunder introduced in the 90th minute would undo all their work. It would essentially be walking the world's longest tightrope. But if they could pull it off, they would bring some never-before-seen creature into existence.

This is exactly what Aleksandr Sokurov did when he made *Russian Ark*. Just one take, longer than any in the history of cinema. This is barbarism, a return to film's Pleistocene beginnings. Ninety-six minutes without a single cut. Most films require hundreds of hours of material, vast amounts of images that are then laboriously sliced and arranged into 90-minute stories. Post-production editing is where film acquires its grammar, goes from being an assemblage of grunts and clicks into a proper language. But *Russian Ark* does not have any of this. To compensate for this self-imposed aphasia, Sokurov took unprecedented control over everything around his camera. He traced for it a two-kilometer path through Russia's most majestic museum, and then he made legions of actors practice along that path for months. He took utmost care that every tiny detail that his camera might encounter was strictly controlled and accounted for.

Somewhere in this mad endeavor Aleksandr Sokurov endowed film with something it never expected to have: the aura of the original.

Walter Benjamin: "The stripping of the veil from the object, the destruction of the aura, is the signature of a perception whose 'sense for all that is the same in the world' has so increased that, by means of reproduction, it extracts sameness even from what is unique."

The right to hold reproductions in our hands has become an unquestioned part of life, our ability to make copies at will is now a basic part of technological literacy. When Benjamin originated the idea of the "aura," he was writing about the effects that photography would have on our sense of the original; but even more than photography, film has no original, it is just an endless string of reproductions tracing back in on themselves. It is by necessity a more collective effort than any other art. The apparatus required to create one has grown to the point that we now routinely see films backed by hundreds of millions of dollars spewed from enormous, multi-national corporate entities. The vision of reality claimed by such films is a mass, homogenized vision of reality. Lacking any trace of the unforeseen, such films have no aura, could not possibly have it, because they are explicitly, implacably engineered to give us the experience that we expect to have. But Sokurov's film is the opposite. Its very nature guarantees that it will show us something unique in the history of cinema. It is not a spliced assemblage of thousands of takes, it has an original: those events that took place for 96 minutes in the Hermitage Museum. It will be different, but will it be any good? Will it speak nonsense to us, or will it tell us something worth hearing?

Aleksandr Sokurov had the Hermitage Museum at his disposal for precisely one day. There was time enough for three tries. The first two were deemed failures and broken off before they could be completed. The third try was subsequently released as the film *Russian Ark*. Did they get it right on the third try? It is the very same reason that makes this question nonsense that ensures *Russian Ark* contains the aura.

Tarkovsky: "I reject the principles of 'montage cinema' because they do not allow a film to continue beyond the edges of the screen: they do not allow the audience to bring personal experience to bear on what is in front of them on film."

We begin shrouded in the black of death. Sokurov, who is doing the narration behind journeyman Steadicam handler Tilman Büttner, says there was an accident, or an explosion, something—he doesn't know where he is or how he got there. Were this a typical film, the camera's blackness would now dissolve to reveal the anxious eyes of loved ones looking down at us on a hospital gurney, but instead the blackness gives way to a snowscape in which we find sumptuously dressed women and their men. They look like they've come out of the 19th century. They are entering a grand building.

It is not immediately apparent that we're in a point of view shot, because no one is reacting to the camera being here. There's no sense that anyone can "see" the camera, which is usually how we figure out we're in a POV shot. This feeling of looking through the camera would normally give me the convincing sensation of being in the film, but *Russian Ark* feels different, its subtly discomfiting weirdness estranges me at the same time as I'm drawn in. I only know that I'm seeing through the camera because of Sokurov's running monologue, which is a somewhat nervous babbling of whatever he happens to be thinking. "Is all this being staged for me?," he asks. "Am I to play a role? What kind of play is this?" Not questions we generally ever ask ourselves. These are questions of confusion, questions of complete disorientation. He doesn't even know if he's alive or dead. Sokurov's confusion pulls me into his film-long search for the role he is supposed to be playing.

Essentially it's a director playing a spectator within his own movie. What else could a camera do for 96 minutes but wander and observe? Cameras are, by definition, unblinking eyeballs. They don't have hands to grab things with, they don't have mouths for talking. All they're capable of is looking. So it makes sense that Sokurov's film is about him wondering and wandering. It's a little reminiscent of film noir—detectives are essentially spectators in another person's world—but a noir pulls in to a final pit of certainty, whereas *Russian Ark* is blessed with an intriguing air of continual expansion. It has no plot, its only movement is to further embellish this spectacle that Sokurov is walking through. A theatrical spectacle: Sokurov brings up theater continually throughout the film. Early on he declares, "Russia is like a theater." In one remarkable set-piece he walks through a hellish backstage, with rat-like flymen scurrying around the infernal machines that create the on-stage artifice. Sokurov is damning us to remember: film is just a projected image, but theater is real people.

The acting in a theater never feels as real to me as it does in film. People in a play need to project their role all the way to the cheap seats: they use exaggerated gestures, and they yell so loud that I can see the spit fly from their mouth. The stage never quite stops being a stage. But film can leverage all of the thousands of hours of video recording that I've already watched to convince me that it is real. Directors can film on location. They can request take after take until the actors really are living their roles.

Russian Ark upends this. It feels to me like a play. Like any theatrical actor, Sokurov requires the first few minutes of the film to slip into character. These are the confused first minutes when he keeps muttering about his role in the film. I acclimate to the film's unfamiliar rhythms in tandem with Sokurov, like an audience warming up with its players. I can feel the aura getting started. It's the thrill of not quite knowing what's meant to happen, what's not.

Hélène Cixous: "We don't have the last word: truth always has the word before, and we run out of breath at its heels."

Sokurov has hardly gotten his wits about him when he meets the Marquis de Custine, a real-life 19th-century aristocrat who knows exactly as much about what he's doing here as does Sokurov. They decide to wander together, although their alliance remains a loose one. Sokurov seems to be the saturnine of the pair, trudging along, observing, making pithy Slavic remarks. The Marquis is aloof and mercurial, the kind of aging vanity who will be confiding in you one moment and then rushing off to pick up the handkerchief of a willowy young woman. He actually did visit Russia in 1839, he even wrote a well-received travelogue about it. He judged Russia rather harshly, calling it a copy of European civilization (it seem that this struck a nerve). In *Russian Ark* he is true-to-form, goading Sokurov to admit that his beloved Hermitage is a knock-off of the Vatican. He says rather insultingly, "Are you interested in beauty or just its representation?"

It's a potent question for a filmmaker to pose to himself. Can film really offer us beauty, and not merely the representation of beauty? How does it slip off a film's surface to exist within us?

Stanley Cavell: "Only art itself can discover its possibilities, and the discovery of a new possibility is the discovery of a new medium."

One answer: right around minute 30, Sokurov and the Marquis come upon a blind woman admiring the art in the Hermitage. Clearly she's not here for the representation of beauty, she's wants something else, call it aura. The Marquis makes friends with her, and she declares that she wants to show him Rubens' "The Feast in the House of Simon the Pharisee." He plays a cruel trick. First he tells her that the painting is not in the gallery, and then, after walking up to it and admiring it himself, he announces that he has found it. But instead of showing the woman that painting, he points her in the opposite direction. The trusting woman smiles and basks in what she thinks is the Rubens. What does she see in this moment? And am I so wrong for thinking that a few minutes later, when the Marquis kneels down before a portrait of Peter and Paul and crosses himself with religious fervor, he is just as blind to that painting as art? Standing next to him is a young modern man who knows nothing of religion—maybe he's a nihilist—and he tells the Marquis that he looks at Peter and Paul because he "likes them," as though they were just two people someone decided to paint. This slight, poetic young man ventures to tell the Marquis that one day all men will become like him, and the Marquis seethes back: How can you know what will become of men if you have not read the scriptures? He makes as if to strike the young man, who shrinks in terror.

Could the difference between these men's approach to art be more stark? The Marquis is a man of his times, that is to say, he insults Wagner, he praises the Vatican as the most beautiful structure on Earth. The modern young man carries no religious affiliation, for him art can be disconnected from God. It carries its own light—whereas, when the Marquis looks at the painting, the devotion he feels comes from the reflected light of the scriptures. We begin to see now why he played that cruel trick on the blind woman, why he bodily threatens this young man. His concept of art is bounded by a sense of representation, the aura for him is not inherent in the work, it is God. But for the moderns, the Original. We are a little like the blind woman, being led around by the forces of myth and fame to stare not at the image but at its reputation. Beauty in art can be a devout stare at a biblical scene, it can be adoration of mystery, it can be a lunge toward what is. If Sokurov sees beauty at all, he sees it as the misty, subliming horizon toward which he longingly stares at the end of the movie, when, looking through a window at the limits of his ark—the only frame *through* which he stares in the whole film—he realizes that he is but a pearl adrift on a vast ocean.

Lacan: "The whole truth is what cannot be told."

Shortly after the incident with the Rubens, Sokurov and the Marquis come upon a door. It looks just like any other door, but somehow Sokurov knows it's forbidden. He tries to warn the Marquis off, but the stubborn man steps through. It is a dark, cavernous room littered with the remnants of thousands of wooden frames. Their paintings are nowhere to be seen. The Marquis is called forth by a burly, hammering man; it's the siege of Stalingrad, and he's building the frames into coffins. All at once the sacredness that the Marquis has always found in art is made all-too concrete, while at the same time we see that Sokurov

74

has, literally, broken the frame entirely, has revealed it as a home for dead matter. Horrified, he backs away. *His* camera frame will hold no dead representations. It is light and life.

And here is the weirdest thing about this bizarre scene that occurs in the exact chronological center of *Russian Ark*: the coffin-maker accuses the Marquis of stepping on the corpses of dead men, corpses that we do not see but that the man sees quite well. This is particularly jarring, because Sokurov and the Marquis seem like ghosts: most of the people they encounter in the Hermitage don't see or react to them in any way at all. But now, it is they who cannot see or react to these corpses. The movie has inverted itself: the belief that I have crept as ghosts through the Hermitage with these two men is ruptured. Is this man the real ghost? Or is he just mad with hunger and anxiety? Either way, Sokurov has made me doubt my eyes. Am I seeing representations, or am I seeing truths?

Soon after the scene with the coffin-maker, Sokurov and his friend walk into the middle of an enormous imperial reception, complete with palace guards, a captive audience of hundreds, and royalty. It is something out of a gigantic 19th-century canvas, as though the two men have finally entered the paintings they have been admiring. Sokurov treats this scene like a theater's stage: there are hundreds of spectators standing on the sidelines and watching the unfolding of a drama between Tsar Nicholas I and the Shah of Iran's grandson. The event is as scripted as any performance, with all the dignitaries acting out roles. And indeed, if this is a play, then it is one that the aristocratic audience has seen many times before, that era's equivalent of the re-run. After wandering through the action for a couple of minutes (nobody can see the men, who are once again ghosts), Sokurov turns his attentions to the wearied bystanders, who seem more interested in gossip and one another's gowns than the hours of imperial pomp that are in store for them. Still some do watch—hoping for what? For the shocking, reality-inducing misstep that I have hoped to see for 50-some minutes? A newsworthy accident, something to prove that the world before them is permeable? Something not so horrible as a tragedy, but also more than just a gaffe—something in between, which, like art, does not break reality but tears it just a tiny bit, so that we can have enough room to look past the frame of our world and see it anew.

This scene, the most scripted in the film, is also the one where the aura is most potent. For the past hour Sokurov has been conditioning me to be unsure of when the actors in this film can see him and when they cannot. There's no logic to it—some of the characters see Sokurov and the Marquis and some don't. At times it even happens that someone who couldn't originally see them suddenly does. This unreliability is one thing among crowds in public spaces. But now, at the acme of the Russian Empire and amid a wobbly balance between the vanities of two civilizations, Sokurov and the Marquis are wandering through with their mouths open. The immaculate and lavish attendees are constantly glancing into the camera, and I am staring back, I am looking hard to see *if they see me*. It is a little like the eerie, belated exchange that takes place when you look at a picture you've taken, and there on the sidelines is someone's small, forgotten face frowning into your lens. Or rather, it's like when seeing a play at a small theater, the actors and I are so close together that I believe they feel my individual gaze on them. This is a moment that blends spectator and voyeur, the person who has a right to look and the person who looks in spite of not being allowed to. At times these actors stare into my eyes and I am thrown all out of balance: do I stare back as per my right as paid spectator, or do I succumb to the chastened feeling of the found voyeur and look away? When I wondered if that actor saw me sleeping during his performance, we entered into a rudimentary sort of relationship. You can have this relationship with a theatrical performance. You can even have it with a painting—remember how they say the Mona Lisa's eyes follow you? But *Russian Ark* is the only time in memory that I have felt it with a film. Right here in Tsar Nicholas I's mammoth reception chamber, I am having it with these scores of Russians standing in nice, tidy lines, as their gaze drifts from their tsar into Sokurov's camera—that is, onto me. Am I foolish for wanting to look down into my lap? Or am I seeing now that Sokurov is not merely concerned with the representation of beauty? Have I become that mistake that mars *their* script, have I become the film's proof of reality to itself?

D.H. Lawrence: "I always remember meeting the eyes of a gipsy woman, for a moment, in a crowd, in England. She knew, and I knew. What did we know! I was not able to make that out. But we knew."

There is so much gazing in this film, what did we spend all our time looking at before the invention of screens? How did I begin to see art differently once I knew I could find it in a Google search, how did men and women begin to see each other differently once their exchanges were supplemented with social media profiles? An era of screens gives so much more to gaze at that the spectacle loses its authority to command attention. So then what has taken spectacle's place? *Russian Ark* invites me to consider what has been deemed worth looking at over time and how that has changed. Sokurov collapses them into a film that is both cinematic and theatrical. It all flies together in this scene in which the Tsar apologizes to the Shah.

From one kind of imperial pomp to another, the film concludes with an enormous ball, complete with a live orchestra, hundreds of dancers, all the stuff of real life, as though Sokurov had filmed actual people going about their day. Sokurov is wandering, the orchestra is playing, people are dancing the waltz, that most theatrical of dances, and who can say if anyone is any longer acting for the camera, if they would have played these roles any differently had Sokurov not been there to record them doing so. This culminating spectacle feels right, and it is here that the Marquis tells Sokurov that he has decided to stay. He will stand still instead of continuing "forward" with Sokurov. But what precisely does that leave his status as?

The ball ends, a huge rush toward the exits, Sokurov washed along by thousands of extras—it looks precisely like the aftermath of a successful opera, or a gala film premiere. We have all known this moment when, artifice ending, we stand up from our seats, unstiffen our joints, the lights gently ignite and we can still feel within our skins the lingering effects of the representations we have just witnessed; perhaps there is a tear or two on our cheeks, we feel art's fading sway as we begin to step back into the unmediated, unnarrated, unedited world. In these moments I know that the aura is an effect of art, as are many of the emotions I am destined to feel in a life that is, it must be admitted, much less full of drama, ecstasy, pain, discovery, and horror than the art I regularly enjoy. There is a term for when we experience the aura in our own lives, it is called *the uncanny*, it is reserved it for those moments when life *makes a mistake*, that is, when it begins to take on the qualities that Sokurov has found expression for in his film.

Russian Ark concludes with a beautiful plunge backwards as Sokurov skims down the middle of the departing crowd—is he on wheels?—we may fleetingly examine the faces of people one last time as they make their exit from art's domain and into the real world. But still we remain within the Hermitage, as always, though there is a sense of stepping outside, of leaving the theater, even though we are still indoors. At long last Sokurov finds the perimeter of his mammoth, 96-minute shot. He steps up to a window through which a cold mist draws, he looks out and sees a dark, stormy, frigid ocean. It appears as though the polar ice cap is peacefully releasing itself up into space. He tells us there is no end. A final reminder of the artificiality of any story—whether seen at the movies or created to make sense of our own life—of the fact that we are condemned to gaze in search of completion, of aura, of art and meaning—of beauty—that to do so we must assume roles we are ill-fit to play, but that to do otherwise would not be human.

2004, TALKING TO HIMSELF

The Five Obstructions, Lars Von Trier (2003)

If ever there were a well-meaning, fallible filmmaker who just couldn't find the right human being to share his demons with, it would be Lars von Trier. I am both riveted and appalled by his films. He's a genius with a camera, but he's also the absolute king of digging out someone's heart with a coffee spoon and making a complete mess of it. You won't hear me admit much sympathy for Lars, but I think that must be a very lonely thing: always wanting to share feelings with someone and always turning it into a bloody mess—and not only that, but in so doing making everyone think you're a complete asshole.

I don't think Lars is a complete asshole. I think he's just Lars, as fallible and in need of love as any of us, and maybe a little too oafish in imposing his will on others. I feel privileged to make all these rather excessive statements about the personal life of a man I've never met because Lars once dramatized these shortcomings in a film about friendships and conversations. It was a very good film, in fact. It's called *The Five Obstructions.*

The basis of this film is Lars' idea: "I'm going to help Jørgen Leth." I don't know exactly why Lars thinks Jørgen needs his help; the film never makes it clear what he believes is Jørgen's problem, nor why he's the one to solve it. It seems to have something to do with Jørgen's inability to be honest with himself about who he is, and Lars' pathological need to tell everyone—himself included—just what's wrong with them. He tends to do this by picking on them with insult after insult until they're forced to scream out the truth.

Jørgen is Lars' cinematic mentor. He's the creator of a short film called "The Perfect Human" that Lars absolutely venerates—he's seen it some 20 times. Lars' way to help Jørgen is by challenging him to remake "The Perfect Human" five times. He's going to have a conversation with Jørgen through this process. The truth-inducing insult he'll deliver is that he gets to impose whatever ridiculous conditions he wants on Jørgen's remakes. These challenges are going to get his mentor to reach some catharsis—although no matter how many times I watch *The Five Obstructions* I never really get what Lars expects to happen after that. Is catharsis just an end of its own? Is this a prelude to some kind of healing? Or maybe it's just Lars' ego running amok again.

D.H. Lawrence: "No two persons can meet at more than a few points, consciously. If two people can just be together fairly often, so that the presence of each is a sort of balance to the other, that is the basis of the perfect relationship."

Lars' little project always reminds me of "The Hunger Artist," Kafka's infamous story about a man whose art is in starving himself. He just sits in a cage and doesn't eat, and the people who watch him find some kind of beauty in it. This is art. It's popular to think of art as this potted flower that must be nurtured with unceasing enthusiasm and Guggenheim fellowships, but Kafka tells us that it's not so fragile. You couldn't kill your art if you wanted to. To the contrary—your art is precisely what kills you. You can't even really share it with anyone: it's a lonely little cage that people watch you through.

I'm inclined to go with Kafka on this one. I'm big enough to grant you your own idea of art, but I will always side with those who feel the ache of Kafka's hunger. I feel this ache, and I've found it to be good for very little, except perhaps instilling a drive toward truth, which is the most important thing. I'd say Lars feels this drive too much for his own good. He'd certainly be much happier if he didn't have to follow his hunger, not that that's an option. No, I'd say his best option is the one Sigmund

Freud offered us: art as psychotherapy. Not the flower that we currently patronize it as, and not Kafka's tapeworm; something more like a mirror for peering into your soul. Art as therapy. No. Art as dialectic. Better. Art as *conversation*.

The Five Obstructions begins by shoving you right into the midst of Lars and Jørgen's conversation. There's Jørgen with his hair oddly short and those two ever so slightly bucked front teeth that pop out like flags whenever he smiles. There's Lars, head shaved, little pockets of stubble oddly dispersed around his face, looking like the kind of person he would cast as an Eastern European criminal. The camera is tight on them, the angles are all skewed, there's all kinds of miscellaneous junk in the background. This is the cinematic equivalent of that living room clutter that you keep trying to hide when you have people over.

In other words, it's a Dogme95 film. This is what I love about Lars—only someone of his sensibility could have come up with Dogme95. And that's because he doesn't try to hide the shit. You know the shit exists, I know the shit exists, Lars certainly knows the shit exists. So okay. Let's stop trying to pretend it's not there, and let's talk about it.

And what a glorious way to talk about shit: we're going to remake "The Perfect Human" five times, says Lars, with a little mischievous look on his face. I've never really figured out why Lars *loves* "The Perfect Human" so much. This is a bizarre, 17-minute film that Jørgen made in 1967, a kind of pseudo-documentary where he films the "perfect" man and the "perfect" woman doing everyday things like trimming their nails and brushing their hair and walking around their infinite little room. There's a voice-over where the narrator makes naïve remarks regarding his curiosity toward their perfect nature, talking as if they're caged animals. The set is spotlessly white, and the "perfect" man and "perfect" woman are all-around embodiments of not-a-spot-of-lint-ness. Every time I watch the film, it makes me think of a very well-tended, very, very clean mental hospital.

As Lars and Jørgen watch the film on Lars' sad little television set, I have to ask myself, What exactly makes Claus Nissen the perfect man? One day as I watched him dancing around in a tuxedo against a background white as infinity, it hit me: he's annoying as hell. He's just dancing around the frame with some hip little sunglasses on, smiling at me like he knows something I'll never figure out, clearly aware that the camera is on *him* and not on *me*, because the camera is drawn to beauty and symmetry and normalcy, and he knows that he's all those things and I'm not. He's perfect because he's just happy to be dancing there, perfectly inhabiting his body with a satisfaction that only the gods and movie actors could ever know. And this complete satisfaction with the fact of being oneself is hugely, *hugely* annoying—this is just what being the perfect human is. I want to punch him in the face. I bet Lars would like to punch Claus Nissen in the face too.

Mary Ruefle: "Nothing I understand haunts me. Only the things I do not understand have that power over me."

Lars and Jørgen are not perfect humans. They don't inhabit a perfect white, infinite room, they inhabit Lars' disheveled little workspace where he keeps pouring himself more white wine and it's obvious he still has a drinking problem. Jørgen and Lars are both depressives who have done a lot of bad things in the name of themselves, and they'll probably keep doing somewhat bad things all their lives. Lars in particular seems like he'd be a handful. For one thing, he can't stop talking about everything he thinks is wrong with himself. He's one of those people who turn trauma into a heroic personal attribute and just shove it up your nose until you can't breathe. Jørgen on the other hand is that monolith of a friend whose psychological depths you're never going to tap. I can see the grey in their hair, but the mannerisms and behavior are that of boys. Overgrown boys. These boys certainly have personality issues, and they're essentially feeding their egos in making a movie about themselves making movies, but out of all these bits and scraps of self-indulgence comes something truly interesting, and interesting to watch. One begins to get a sense of why artists are driven to make art, and why any non-artist should give a damn about what they make.

With obvious relish Lars lays out the first set of obstructions:

1. No edit will be longer than 12 frames.
2. Jørgen will answer meaningless rhetorical questions he posed in the original film.
3. It will be shot in Cuba.
4. Jørgen will not be permitted to build a set.

The idea of constraint in art is by now a rather old glove. It received its full due in '60s France—an unrestrained place if ever there was one—where a group of writers, of male writers mind you (Dogme95 is a little boys' club too), got together and decided to form a treehouse that they were going to call the Ouvroir de littérature potentielle, the workshop of potential literature. And what were to be the tools in this workshop? Constraints. Weird little rules that they set themselves before writing. By far the best-known of these is Georges Perec's injunction against himself to ever use the letter *e* in his book *La Disparition (A Void)*, which he then wrote as an existential fairy tale about a search for the missing "Anton Vowl." Lars reportedly made Dogme95, his own workshop of potential films, in just 25 minutes. He said he couldn't stop laughing the whole time. And at the end of that humorous half-hour he had a "vow of chastity" restricting filmmakers to a series of rules, mostly to do with limiting the scope and technology of the project: filming must be done on location; props and sets must not be brought in; only diegetic sound; handheld cameras; no special lighting; etc.

Robert Bresson: "Sudden rise of my film when I improvise, decline when I execute."

Dogme95 is a kind of banalization of art, a limiting of its means until what is most likely to come out is, in Lars' inimitable word, "crap." (I've watched plenty of Dogme95 films and can verify this.) Even when Lars isn't shooting per Dogme95 standards, he still goes out of his way to make his films ugly and unnecessarily restricted and downright banal. But what comes from this method—at least in his hands—isn't crap. Or rather, it is and it isn't. The Modernist art movement was largely a movement based on discovering the aesthetic potential of crap. So, obviously, Duchamp sticking a urinal on a pedestal and calling it art. And ever since that day, Modernist art has been dogged by people with no sense of humor decrying it for trying to explore the banal. Thus the guy who sneers at a Jackson Pollock because his son could have made it. Incidentally, you have to understand that when I use the word *crap* here, I'm using it in a very broad sense, everything from the trash that gets taken away every Wednesday to the kitsch sitting on grandmother's shelves to all those sharp little unwanted thoughts embedded just behind my eyes. This is the subject that the Modernists chose to explore—and why wouldn't they? There's no single thing the modern world has produced in such abundance as crap. The production, consumption, and disposal of crap is the purpose of capitalism. All this crap that sits beneath capitalism is the very submerged iceberg of our way of life, and if there's one thing Lars has proven his interest in, it's forcing this truth into the light. His career as a filmmaker has been a terminal drive deeper and deeper into that immense mound of crap we live atop. And in doing this, Lars is being pathologically honest about us. We all have crap, we all have it in essentially the same few complexes, we all medicate it with the same few substances and activities. It is the *lingua franca* of our culture, and it is precisely what Lars is trying to make this film—*every* film—about.

So Lars is saying to Jørgen, *Let's try to explore all that crap in your head*, and Jørgen is saying right back, *No*. My favorite scene from the making of this first remake comes when Jørgen is treading crystal-clear blue water in his Havana hotel pool. It's a very brief shot, just long enough for a shirtless Jørgen to utter the following words: "twelve frames are a paper tiger." Such satisfaction as he says those words! This shot is the mate of one that occurs about ten minutes earlier, when Lars lays down the 12-frame obstruction and we see a shot of Jørgen's face where it looks like that cigar he's smoking just went in the wrong end. But now Jørgen conquers Lars, he's made this first remake despite all of Lars' obstructions, and here, for just a moment, he inhabits that pool just as he is meant to inhabit it, like an actor who has finally come to live his role on screen. This is perfection, and Jørgen obviously loves it. I do not, and nor do I think does Lars, either. When I have known this sensation of perfectly inhabiting my identity, it's filled me with dread, like standing atop a tiny ledge at the pinnacle of an enormous pyramid. All it takes is the lightest touch to send me tumbling down.

A few things you might not know about Lars: he's so afraid of flying that he's never been to the United States, despite making two films that are set in it and very critical of it; for years he drove from Denmark to France for Cannes, until, in 2011, after he expressed sympathy for Hitler, he was banned indefinitely from the festival; he's filmed live sex in a number of "female-friendly" porn films he made in the late '90s, which reportedly led Norway to legalize pornography in 2006; he has a way of making actors declare that they'll never make another movie after they've worked with him; his parents were nudists and took him to nudist camps.

They also didn't believe in setting rules for children.

The Five Obstructions was the first film of Lars' that I ever watched. I saw it as part of the 2004 San Francisco International Film Festival—the second year I attended—in the old, shed-like Pacific Film Archive. I have a very particular history with the PFA. It was the place where I first saw Hitchcock—*The 39 Steps*—which was also one of my first dates with the woman with whom I would eventually see *Suzhou River*, and who accompanied me on *The Five Obstructions* and led to my viewing of so many other films in this book. It was the place where I would discover most of the directors I now regard as canonical, the place where I audited UC Berkeley's Film 50 class and learned about cinematic history and technique. Without the influence of the PFA in my life, I don't see how this book could have been written. An abbreviated list of the directors I first saw there would include the aforementioned Hitchcock and Lars, as well as Yasujirō Ozu, Claude Lanzmann, Frederick Wiseman, D.W. Griffiths, Sergei Eisenstein, Max Ophüls, Robert Wiene, F.W. Murnau, Pasolini, Eric Rohmer, Agnes Varda, Jia Zhangke, Kurosawa, Marcel Pagnol, Chris Marker, Jacques Tati, Grant Gee, Pedro Costa, Robert Altman, Kenji Mizoguchi, Ernst Lubitsch, John Ford, Howard Hawks, and Rainer Fassbinder.

So anyway, the film that Jørgen makes in response to Lars' first set of obstructions is fantastic and Lars is dumbfounded by how damn good it is. He tells Jørgen, "one always feels furious when it turns out there are solutions." He gives him caviar and vodka and tells him he's been waiting all morning to have a drink. Always before noon, jokes Jørgen as he takes a sip.

It's here that Lars reveals to Jørgen his secret agenda, that these obstructions are meant to be therapy. Lars doesn't give a damn about Jørgen making good films. Point blank he says he wants him to make "crap."

"I want to banalize you," he says.

If you watch Lars' films, you'll see that he loves the idea of ruining oneself as a way to understand one's demons. Lars himself has been in and out of therapy for years. At least since his second film, 1987's *Epidemic*, he's explicitly said he makes films to cure his depression, and virtually everything since could be considered as a very brutal kind of autopsychoanalysis. Lars knows he'll never be a normal, moderately happy human, so he makes a farce of the pursuit for normalcy. Almost as a challenge, in each film he bears right down on the banal, and inevitably he always ends up swerving into the sublime. This is Lars' particular genius as a filmmaker, and this is precisely what he plans on *The Five Obstructions* being for Jørgen. The very perfection of Jørgen's art is hurting Jørgen—the only way to help him is to force him to ruin it.

Alberto Giacometti: "I do not know whether I work in order to make something or in order to know why I cannot make what I would like to make."

For the second obstruction, Lars tells Jørgen to make a film somewhere where he'll feel completely uncomfortable. As an example, Lars says Jørgen might ironize a dying child in a refugee camp.

I'm not that perverse, replies Jørgen. *Like you*, I can hear him add.

The essence of it: Lars wants to get Jørgen to do something that he's never going to do. As the men haggle over this thing Lars is going to get Jørgen to do one way or another, the next set of obstructions come out:

1. Go into the most miserable place you can think of.
2. Don't show that place in your film.
3. Jørgen has to play the perfect human in this location.
4. The scene he will remake is the meal scene.

Lars is getting personal with this second set of obstructions. The first four were all obstructions in the sense of hurdles: they were meant to make it physically difficult for Jørgen to complete his task. But these are of a different order entirely—they're mindfucks. This is a subject Lars excels at to a rare degree. My guess is that he can't help but mess with the minds of people he's close to.

I, for one, would not want Lars trying to mess with my mind.

Jørgen's second film is a cop-out: he flies to Bombay, finds a slum, and eats the fish dinner with a transparent screen behind him, beyond which you can see vaguely impoverished Indian citizens looking confused and somewhat bored. This is a complete dismissal of Lars' second rule—don't show it. Lars' idea was that Jørgen was going to go and soak up the misery of this place he had sentenced himself to, and then he was going to sublimate it through his consumption of the meal, and it was going to be some godawful Jørgen-style trainwreck. But Jørgen won't let so much as a breath of air inside of him, certainly not the pain and suffering of complete strangers, so instead we see a bunch of confused people through a screen, and Jørgen never gives any indication that he even realizes that they're there. It's another perfectly acceptable film, real capital-A Art, and Lars is incensed because it means that once again Jørgen hasn't so much as flirted with banality. What I would say he's done, what he does with each of the six perfect humans, is he skims the smooth surface of art. He handles this film as coolly and efficiently as he's probably handled every last thing in his life. But still, Jørgen shows us something here, perhaps without realizing it: that screen is how he sees the world. It's the distance between him and Lars, between him and those Indians, between him and every other thing on Earth. Lars is right: the man has placed a tiny little perimeter of infinity all around him. You can see it every time those two big front teeth emerge in one of his impenetrable smiles.

After they watch the second remake Lars is very displeased with Jørgen. He goes from playing the loving God to the vengeful one. I get the idea this is something that happens a lot with Lars. People who place themselves under Lars' direction somehow transgress the rules he has constructed for them and—boom! Vengeful Lars. Just like the Christian God, Lars' punishment for Jørgen comes in the form of a choice: either go back to Bombay and remake the film the way I told you, or make a film with no strings attached whatsoever.

Jørgen looks aghast: "I'd rather have something to hang on to."

We subsequently see Jørgen walking around a hotel in Brussels, the simple predicament of being unable to find one's room turned into a claustrophobic, existential dilemma. I'll bet anything that Lars cut this scene, because this is so utterly Lars: making a dull little predicament that everyone has been through at least once into a vertigo. There's a great shot of Jørgen staring out to the left of the frame while, behind him, a hotel corridor drifts off in rectilinear perspective. This is exactly the corridor toward our self that none of us will ever finish traveling, the inexhaustible corridor toward the truth that Lars traverses untiringly. But you see, Jørgen is staring out away from it, not the least bit interested in traveling down it.

The bizarre thing about remake number three is that it stars, as the perfect human, a 65-year-old Patrick Bauchau—36 years after he starred in Eric Rohmer's film *La Collectionneuse*. I absolutely love *La Collectionneuse*. And Jørgen loves it too! He calls it "Rohmer's most important film." Whatever does he mean by that? Could it be that deep within Jørgen's cold Nordic heart he really does believe in romanticism? Or maybe he just found the disturbingly pre-pubescent body of a 20-year-old Haydée Politoff . . . inspiring. The truth is that Jørgen has fucked lots of suspiciously young women in all kinds of Third World locales. He even, at the ripe old age of 73, made a film about it called *The Erotic Man*.

It was not received well. Although as Jørgen noted rather enthusiastically on his blog, the "very satisfying premiere" featured "no walk-outs!"

But anyway, Patrick Bauchau. Now this is a strange choice. Claus Nissen was a sweet, doddering oaf who took a child-like satisfaction in doing things like smoking a pipe, tying his shoes, and walking back and forth. I don't think Patrick Bauchau would be caught dead smoking a pipe instead of a cigarette, but if he did he certainly wouldn't be capable of putting that pipe in his mouth without making it into a sexual proposition. Perfect human version Patrick Bauchau is a sexually predatory, elegant macho trotting around with a gun in his briefcase. Perfect human version Claus Nissen is an asexual manboy in a little white sanatorium, chaste as a Ken doll.

"Not a mark has been left on you," says Lars to Jørgen, and Jørgen looks back at him with a rich, disdainful smile. You can almost hear him saying, what crap, Lars, what godawful nonsense. Jørgen wants nothing of the kind of emotional vivisection Lars does by pure instinct; it freaks him out. Jørgen's strength is giving the appearance of doing what Lars actually does. Lars tells him to go root through the crap, and each time Jørgen makes something perfect in its hermeticism. Impermeability is Jørgen's image of perfection, an impermeability that you've convinced yourself is more than porous enough. And this, really, is Jørgen's inability to ever so much as flirt with the banal, because Jørgen is not a man of pores, he's a man of sleek, smooth surfaces. Lars is going to push with all his might to break through, and Jørgen is content with making a mockery of the whole venture.

I must admit, my own innate sympathies will always be with dead-end truth-tellers like Lars, because I've lived my life with that ache for self-knowledge. I have no idea what I'm here for if not to feel this ache. This is surely banal to anybody who doesn't feel it, but it is mine, it's my hunger, it's what I have to feed. And so I do it. I see quite well why Lars can't stand Jørgen's impermeability, even if Jørgen is being a rather good sport. He wants Jørgen to feel this ache for self-knowledge, but it's just not who he is. And so I feel bad for Lars, always trying to force his friend open and always failing. It's becoming clear that Jørgen's getting bored with the whole thing. Lars tells him that he wants to see those last crumbs forced out, those last things that no one wants, and Jørgen just replies, yeah, yeah, whatever. I want you to feel like a turtle on his back, advises Lars. Right, turtle, says Jørgen, let me write that down.

I'm going to make a very, very, very, very simple rule for the next obstruction, says Lars. And I can't imagine it'll be anything but crap.

The fourth obstruction is that Jørgen must make a cartoon.

Both men make it clear that they despise cartoons.

Lars has gone all out. This is total war. Crap by any means necessary.

"I think it's an interesting exercise, actually," Jørgen says, safely ensconced in his beloved Haiti. What confidence! You can see that he's already figured out how to impose that cruel distance, once again he's gotten beyond the frame of his own creation and has become the cool, detached observer. Jørgen is perfect. It's clear that he's discovered how to impose a masterful defense that Lars will never breach. The game is over.

What Jørgen does for this fourth film, and I think this is complete cheating, what Jørgen does is to hire a cartoonist living in Texas to do all the work for him. Jørgen just tells him what he likes and what he doesn't. We can't help looking for a solution that satisfies us, says Jørgen. A solution to a problem. This is always Jørgen's approach.

This fourth remake is a mélange of Jørgen's first three remakes, plus the original perfect human, and it is here that I can't help but notice something that's been going on the entire movie: these films are becoming more and more self-referential. And this makes sense, because with each new set of obstructions Lars has been digging ever deeper with his insults, Jørgen digging ever deeper into a defense. His defense is brilliant: rather than let the insult force its way into himself, Jørgen is deflecting it onto the films they're co-creating. In other words, if this film is a conversation, then the conversation between Lars and Jørgen is deteriorating. It's becoming one of those degenerative conversations where, instead of arguing about the stuff you're supposed to be arguing about, you start arguing about the language you're using to argue. A meta-argument. *The Five Obstructions* is becoming a commentary on itself.

After they watch the fourth film Lars tells Jørgen he's a tease, and it's true—Jørgen *is* a tease. He knows it! He laughs when he hears Lars call him a tease, because now he's made a freaking cartoon of all things. The two men hang up their phones and Jørgen, who's in Haiti, says very legalistically that

Lars admitted it was a cartoon. Lars sits in his sad, messy little room eating caviar alone with the cartoon image of Jørgen on the television screen behind him.

Paul Valéry: "How often we forget that to stimulate and to satisfy oppose each other!"

After Jørgen makes a perfectly fine cartoon, Lars tells us that he has prepared for this possibility. He has. In the event that Jørgen once again bests Lars, which he's obviously done, even if now he's cheated a *second* time, the final obstruction will be that Jørgen reads a text written by Lars.

In this simple act Lars has terminated the conversation. In other words, he has chosen to go nuclear. This is that moment in the argument when you totally lose your composure by telling off your friend with such an unholy shitstorm of fury that the entire preceding argument is immediately rendered irrelevant. Lars has pulled out the Big Insult, that one thing you shouldn't do unless if you're prepared to face the consequences. And in fact, Lars' Big Insult is extraordinary. Here we have Jørgen credited as the director of a film that consists of him reading a letter that Lars has written, and which Lars has instructed him in how to read. It gets better: this letter is ostensibly Jørgen indicting Lars for being too pushy. This forces us to assume that Lars is now contrite for how he's behaved for the whole of the film and wishes to express his remorse through Jørgen's lips—except that when has Lars ever been contrite for anything? And as an added little cherry of metadiscourse on top, as this letter is read, I, the viewer, see a montage of scenes from the making of *The Five Obstructions*; i.e., all the "evidence" of the crime that Lars has just perpetrated and that he is now "apologizing" for through the mouth of the man he has been wronging.

So in other words, in this final film, the summation of this whole thing called *The Five Obstructions*, Lars and Jørgen are plowing through the crap they've created in the process of making the film up to this point. They've essentially made a pile of crap for the express purpose of digging into that, *instead of* the pre-existing pile of crap they were supposed to be digging into to begin with. So has anything at all been accomplished here?

I think so. In this era of unsurpassed crap, we've turned to making crap about the crap—that is, we're now at the point of diving into the pile atop the pile, all that angsty crap that we can't help but simmer over given the fact of there being so much crap in the world. But the thing is, even if we only ever reach that meta-pile, in a strange way we're actually digging through the pile underneath at the same time. To phrase it all differently, when you're trying to mess with your cinematic mentor's head, what you're really doing at the same time is re-examining that time you messed with the head of that Icelandic actress. And that's one of *The Five Obstructions'* great elegances: it does this in a purely original way that so precious few of our sweating, self-conscious, *unperfect* artists ever manage.

As far as the meta-pile goes, Lars has a quite distinguished and long-standing history. In fact, in the breadth and depth of the people's heads he's attempted to mess—and his inventiveness in doing so—he's almost certainly our most accomplished living filmmaker. Making an entire film about bullying Jørgen is just the beginning. He once sent Björk, who was wrecked by Lars when he directed her in his film *Dancer in the Dark*, a pillow with the words "If I always allow myself the time to feel my feelings, and then tell what I feel, then Lars can't manipulate me." This was after Björk and Lars had conducted a number of little power struggles on the set of *Dancer in the Dark*. She sent the pillow back, and Lars has kept it in his office. Charlotte Gainsbourg, whom Lars has cut off her own clitoris in *Antichrist*, said of him, "I really have the impression that I was playing him, that he was the woman, that he was going through that misery, the physical condition, the panic attacks." He finally got inside of Kirstin Dunst's head after he filmed a scene of her vagina and referred to it as "the beaver shot." He's reputed to have hypnotized a pretty club girl for his second film, *Epidemic*, made her actually think she was seething with carbuncles, and elicited from her the most perfectly blood-curdling performance of his entire career.

I think from this we can conclude that Lars has a history of failing to get others around him to open themselves to his and their hunger, and when that happens he resorts to tricks. Ever since his first brushes with film and Danish culture, Lars has shown himself to be a remarkably petty, remarkably headstrong person who will do what the hell he wants, and you can join him or have him mess your head. Lars knows nothing of authority; he knows Lars, and he's always been himself, even when he was a dumb little kid with some hand-me-down reels of film. And he regards Jørgen as a mentor. There's a story from Lars' past, when as a star student at the National Film School of Denmark he tried to get Jørgen's attention, when of course Jørgen was already a big man of Danish film, and Jørgen completely ignored him. Years later, Lars, by then the terror of Danish cinema, whose avowed purpose was pretty much to shake Denmark's movie industry out of its pathetic complacency, Lars approached Jørgen and made him his mentor. After all, Lars has never met his true father. On her deathbed in 1989, his mother revealed this secret to him, and in a 2009 interview he called it "a bombshell that is still exploding."

"You are guiltless. You are like a little child," Lars says to Jørgen as they head into the studio to make the sixth and final perfect human, starring Jørgen.

Perhaps this is just my own immodestly stupid way of seeing it, but I have a feeling here that Lars finally understands—Jørgen's perfection is impermeability, and this is all Jørgen is ever going to be to him, so he's going to end this conversation by turning Jørgen into a perfect little singularity. Plus, this being Lars, he's going to make Jørgen impermeable in his own little perfectly Lars way: no matter how many times I watch this last remake, I can't decide who's saying what. Are these Jørgen's thoughts, or Lars', or some combination of the two? My opinion keeps changing as Jørgen reads the letter, and then when I watch it again everything switches up. And then, toss on top of that the montage of shots from the preceding 80 minutes of film, plus the fact that I'm actually taking this in via translated subtitles, so I can only really guess at Jørgen's intonations in various stretches, and you can see, it really is a singularity. This final film becomes a text so deep that it makes the man at its center impermeable.

Raul Ruiz: "Copying, invention, and discovery are extremely complex processes which are not necessarily easy to tell apart."

What Lars likes to do is, he likes to end his films by taking you all the way through to the little singularity that the film has been tunneling toward all along, and then pop you out, alone, on the other side in a sea of black as the credits roll. Thus, for instance, his 2011 film, *Melancholia*, which concludes with the destruction of *the entire Earth*. Yes, we see a huge planet run headlong right into our Earth, and then Lars goes to the credits. This is pretty much the physical, imagistic omega point of every ending Lars has ever made. For Lars, these final few seconds before the credits are the ultimate, the degree zero of the story, and after them there is simply nothing left to tell. Nothing. No sequel, no epilogue. That's it. Such is the case in *The Five Obstructions*, whose final few seconds consist of Jørgen reading Lars' words, "this is how the perfect human falls" as a voice-over to footage of Jørgen pretending to fall down. The words themselves are an ironic quote of Jørgen's original "Perfect Human," where these words are said when Claus Nissen falls down—perfectly, of course—which is in itself an irony, because there's obviously no perfect way to fall down. As Lars both calls himself "perfect" and admits to his "fall," both ironically, and both through Jørgen's lips, we see an image of Jørgen falling down, ironically again, filmed way back in Bombay when he was practicing for the role of the perfect human in the second remake. What else can be said? The film has collapsed into itself, it has become an infinitely dense black hole of fallenness, the very embodiment of Lars' too-offensive search for a truth

Jørgen doesn't want to find, a singularity compressed from the very stuff that had once been *The Five Obstructions*, and this moment—obviously—assumes pride of place as the very last thing Lars lets us see before the end credits. There is nothing else left to be said. The conversation has concluded in the same way that should every single successful conversation, argument, and session of therapy. This dialectic has spiraled itself right into a point that tears just a tiny bit through our idea of reality. It has become art.

2005, UNFETTERED
Koyaanisqatsi, Godfrey Reggio and Phillip Glass (1982)

They are in a small metal cone perched 40 floors off the surface of the Earth.

Beneath them 6 million pounds of liquid hydrogen, liquid oxygen, highly refined kerosene, enough energy to burn every light in New York City for an hour. These liquids will ignite. They will scream for exactly 1,025 seconds. In those 17 minutes, the inhabitants of the cone will be thrown 528,000 feet into the air. They will reach outer space. With one last eruption they will be shoved toward the moon.

How many times did my childish eyes stare at such pillars of fire? So many ignitions, so many millions of tons of steel heaved clear off the Earth and into eternity. My eyes locked onto the television every time these fires appeared.

Their cone will sail through the vacuum for three days. The moon's gravity will catch it, and four days after they were hurtled off of the surface of the Earth, they will descend down toward an untouched sphere. They will be the first to reach a place that human eyes have craned toward for millennia.

There is no known time when humans have not strained toward what we cannot reach. We have always struggled further into the desert, higher up the mountain peak, deeper down the oceanic trench. We have always stared toward the stars.

When they step out of their cone and onto the surface of a new world, they will film it. With a sturdy Hasselblad they will take photos.

Why do we always film it? Why do we always take pictures?

Those grainy, unbearably lethargic long-takes of men in spacesuits touching the surface of an alien world, are they not a kind of avant-garde cinema? That bright, blue Earth rising up over the moon's curve, did this view not change the way we see forever?

Can film do these things without us climbing into space?

Edward Burtynsky: "I realized that as you move up . . . things begin to reveal themselves . . . the descriptive power of the elevated point of view becomes so much more interesting than the view from the ground."

Almost nothing in *Koyaanisqatsi* happens at normal cinematic speed, and almost nothing in it is seen from the surface of the Earth. Godfrey Reggio will use extreme slow motion, extreme speed, he will take his camera high into the sky.

It begins in no man's land. A shot of the so-called Holy Ghost panel. Abstruse figures etched thousands of years ago into 200 feet of sheer cliff face. To reach them, a viewer must journey to the remote desert, then an hour-long drive over a dirt road, then a descent of nearly 1,000 feet into a canyon, then a three-mile hike through the burning sun. One of the most remote places in all of North America. The rocks here have not moved an inch in millennia.

The figures dominate the screen, and then they dissolve into a swelling fireball, a snow of debris. The explosion proceeds at such miniscule pace that it takes a minute to register: a rocket igniting. An incredibly tight shot of the rocket's body climbing inch by inch. As it journeys onward, its furious propulsion immolates the frame.

It is the Saturn V rocket that launched a small capsule bearing the first humans to set foot on another world.

When I was small, my family's television set only displayed so many stations. Let's say a dozen. Every one of them stopped when the space shuttle left our small planet. You would turn the dial, and each number showed the same shot of the shuttle riding its pillar into space. And then, when the tiny light had at last vanished from the camera's eye, there was an ad for something like laundry detergent. Everyone went about their day. Humans had walked on the moon, we had dwelled in space. These were settled facts. The emptiness just beyond our atmosphere was growing crowded with trash.

I have never known a world where this most godlike achievement was not routine.

But here, watching *Koyaanisqatsi*, staring at that hellfire ignition for two brooding minutes, now I finally see what an awesome thing it is to flee Earth's gravity. And how perverse. Grandeur—yes—that inferno is extraordinary, so noble. But also grotesque. We are headed to the stars, but what will it do to get us there?

Stanisław Lem: "For technological civilization promises to *correct* man, both his body and his brain, and quite literally to *optimize* his soul."

And as I stare at those ancient etchings, that massive inferno, there is music: solemn, primeval chants, long worshipful chords. It feels like I am kneeling down to pray at altars familiar and archaic.

I have never seen filmic images so centaur with their music. To quote Alex Ross, "there is no more potent example of a score dominating a film." Philip Glass and Godfrey Reggio worked in tandem. Reggio gave Glass images, Glass composed, Reggio responded with more film, Glass responded to that . . . Amid this visual and aural plenty, one hardly even notices that there are no words in *Koyaanisqatsi*, none at all. This is proper, says Reggio, because, "our language is in a state of vast humiliation. It no longer describes the world in which we live."

After the rocket obliterates the frame, the shot dissolves to a parched landscape of stone ululations from horizon to horizon. All is red and empty hermetic land; remote, rugged, inarguably grand, silent in its desolation. Not only are there no humans, it is hard to imagine humans anywhere near these places. The effect is existential, what I imagine it would be to stare over the airless lunar craters.

Minutes pass, the landscapes are becoming less static. Fields of rock turrets become stagnant water under rough cliffs, then glowing fumaroles, sand dunes awash with wind and light. Suddenly a hanging garden perched upon mountainous slabs of rock, a series of lush valleys, skies crammed with bulbous clouds that flow at a brisk pace.

Now shots of lengthening shadows. The screen is beginning to darken, the sun is setting, the night is consuming the huge rock landscape.

A single beam of light from a low sun shines through a cavern. It contains a line of swirling dust, the same churning haze I see when, during the screening of a film, I look back over my shoulder and up toward the projector.

More shots of such light shining into rock crevasses.

There are birds darting through these caverns, their cries echoing off the rock.

It makes me think of the dawn of life, what possibilities existed before humanity came and named every such thing. I think this film wants to reinstate that broadness, to make us imagine that we can give new names. To make a thing we all can respond to, regardless of what culture we inhabit. A film that communicates without language because language is not fit to its expression, that is multiple, that delivers a message with no fixed meaning. A telegram of anagrams. A Delphic prophecy, each abundant breath auguring woe and prosperity.

There is a thing called "the overview effect," reported by astronauts who have escaped the Earth's well. They see the globe hanging there in the blackness of space, the continents and the oceans all available in a single glance, and it irrevocably shifts their understanding of all being. This is what technology can do: it can give us new perches from which to rediscover.

We must be like the men and women on the rockets and gain a new perspective.

Now a long series of clouds transforming through the air. They are so resolutely polymorphous, capable of taking their mass in any direction at any moment. As open was once the land's language, so the unfettered shapes of these clouds.

The bending sprays of a river diving headlong off a cliff face, down down down, crushing magnificently into mist.

From parched stones to waves and clouds. The film has gained a fluid energy. It is dabbling in chaos. The camera has at last lost its sloth. Accelerating, it is cruising over an Edenic ridge hugged with mist. An exhilarating shot skims the surface of a lake valley. The first hints of humanity. Cultivated land, regal Lake Powell formed from the damming of the Colorado River.

Glass's music has turned rapturous. It is girded by lengthy brass chords that evoke the morning sun, the rays of light streaming over the land. It churns with synthesizer phrases in wild pursuit of their own tails. At last come bursts of sound mimicking a deep, satisfying hum.

Righteous music, joyous rhythms mated to the blossoming land, and so it is very upsetting that they continue even as Reggio's camera leaps from a majestic lake vista to massive eruptions of dirt. So incongruous, this music celebrating nature now suddenly the soundtrack to strip mining. And then, all at once, the music catches up with the swerve of the visuals: from elation to ruin, ominous tones now roll over tense, beating basses. There is a dirty, Frankenstein truck with wheels as tall as man hauling coal and seeming to summon a black wind that smothers everything in sight.

In these few seconds the entire beauteous mood of this movie is shattered. No longer the vagrant forces that have built a world of countless direction—now there is a force unlike any other, one that seeks to impose its definition upon this world. At once fecund and pestilent, reverent and profane. It becomes the movie.

Could we ever know what we are if we lacked a clean perspective?

I first screened this movie as part of my movement toward art. I had taken a step when I chanced on *Russian Ark*, and I had taken another when I screened *The Five Obstructions* at a film festival. Then there was *Koyaanisqatsi*, discovered through my interest in Glass, who had been known to me for two years. The newspaper said he was coming to share this thing called *Koyaanisqatsi*, they would project it above him while he and his ensemble played its music. A 90-minute film with no narrative, not even words, shown in a symphony hall above chamber music played exclusively on synthesizers. Who knew of such things? In my mind I feared that it would prove some dippy goof. The decision to stifle my fears felt devout. I would watch this movie, I would make this gesture of faith. I would trust in this poetic stream of images.

A crisp night among thousands, I stepped into the first tier to watch these men and women work. The entry line stretched around the block, and even passersby felt the charge. (They stopped and asked us what was going on here.) And then, once we all were seated, Glass stepped out onto the stage and a woman screamed out that we loved him.

Such a community. Such people. Where had they been?

I was beginning to sketch out the contours of this faith that draws us to the arts.

We become ourselves by what deluges us. Humanity is ritualistic, the world is the sum of our rituals. They are what remain once our caprice and determination abate. We can make our world into whatever we choose—we need only find a way to impose the habit.

Reggio leaves no doubt as to which habit most consumes us: "It's not that we *use* technology. We *live* technology. Technology has become as ubiquitous as the air we breathe."

He might have added that film is the foremost technological art.

Once that baleful truck is covered with its black wind we see a mess of electrical transmission towers. Then a power plant projecting three indomitable spires, stoic and impressive as stone idols, releasing poisonous gasses into the blue sky. Their sapphire, emerald, and jade pools are beautiful.

The music gains energy as the shots move into a montage of mining operations, oil extraction, nuclear explosions. I see work, the endless cycles of labor that have turned the empty Earth into a place fit for modern humans.

One big Joshua tree in the foreground, in the distance a detonation that momentarily burns the entire frame with white, then the light pulls back into itself and becomes a levitating inferno, and then it is just gray death carrying itself into the sky like a mockery of that noble plume that carried us toward the moon.

The rocket and the nuclear bomb.

The next shot, the most jarring one yet: two humans asleep on the beach. A mother and son. So close I can almost smell them. So abrupt, so easy to make me feel flush with humanity.

No instruments but the human voice now, the music has turned to airy, rising arpeggios that conjure angels darting through rolling clouds and yellow beams. The camera pulls back to reveal more beach, more humans, and behind them all a hulking, ignored power station.

And now the first of many princely shots of skyscrapers. The stereotypical office tower, a colossus's mirror of innumerable rectangles stretching into deep sky. We are perched at the monster's paw, craning our necks back and staring up. Ancient, fearsome, familiar, a dead ringer for Stanley Kubrick's monolith, that same trapezoidal shape, that same sensation of gaping up into our destiny. They are the icons of the modern city: were we to disappear in a sudden pestilence, these glass and steel pillars would be the most impressive monuments of our lost civilization. We would be known as the people who built the tall and hollow slabs. Ignorant of where they lead us, we claim our will is theirs. We strew them by the dozens, building a denser and denser civilization than any other imaginable. It is the density of Andreas Gursky, the highest paid photographer of our time, the density of Burtynsky, his colleague. The density of their industrial-scale photographs of manufactured landscapes that pulse and skitter with piercing detail.

Edward Burtynsky: "Over time, it has become more apparent to me that these aren't as much landscapes as they are places that illustrate the systems. . . . The work is about trying to find a way to represent all of the systems that we have created."

Their hypnotic density is the glorious side of the mass world.

A jumbo jet taxiing down the runway, beginning as a shimmering mirage, growing larger and more distinct as it approaches. Another exemplary manifestation of advanced civilization. The very planet dug out, chewed up, reconfigured in our necessity. Our grandest ambition is to pull out the thick of the Earth and throw it far into the sky.

The airplane promises the perfect freedom of the soaring birds, but in reality it moves like the automobile, ordered and restrained to lines and lanes. This is what Reggio makes us see, as do Gursky and Burtynsky, the hidden order, so regular and repeated that it becomes hypnotic.

A shot of endless rows of cars waiting to be bought cuts to endless lines of tanks waiting to be fired.

A montage of air force jets.

Missiles flying through the air and detonating. A chilling close-up of a squat hydrogen bomb, a piggish belly with a boxy tail.

This ugly little thing our most awesome fury.

Ever since the shot of the monument-like skyscraper, Glass's music has been shortening its phrases and growing more frenzied. A feedback cycle pulling ever tighter, it is straining to engorge itself with sound. Swifter, more and more furious, and then—

in a blink the music drops silent. A shot of Manhattan's towers, prodigious clouds mottling the land with their shadows.

A montage of drab fortresses built to stockpile the poor culminates in several clips of buildings tumbling in upon themselves and releasing enormous clouds of dust and debris.

A stop-motion storm engulfing a skyline, the clouds smothering the puny stalks with a fidgety smoothness.

Now suddenly mass society. Thousands sweeping through a train station. Blurry humanity.

After-work mobs overflowing a sidewalk.

The illuminated rectangles of dusk skyscrapers.

A caramel-red sunset.

Night.

From the mouth of a horn bloom low notes. Tranquil, slow music made up of elongated blues. It is that transitional moment, the 9-to-5 done and now the time to replenish lost strength—a rest, a snack, hours at home and within leisure.

We are beginning to see the city's incessant cycles, the impermanent structures that briefly coalesce into an urban identity. Its monuments are hummingbirds and honeybees compared to those great stone towers in the desert. In 100 years that rock will be as though unchanged, and our cities will have made themselves over into such radical things as would look absolutely foreign to our eyes.

Looking down from high, the land is illuminated by cones and cubes of artificial light, greens and blues pouring on the boulevards, pinpricks of yellow everywhere, some reds. Rays and blinks and beams throbbing through at time-lapse speed.

Shot after shot of illuminated cityscapes pulsing with light.

An uncanny shot of the enormous, rocky moon veering behind a window-lit office tower. Its cold celestial arc is smoother and more perfect than any other motion in this film.

As the lights whip through the city the music is gaining

energy. It is becoming louder and more ardent. It is building. And then——

An explosion of activity.

Lines of lightning rushing down the freeways. Revolving doors spinning like centrifuges. Blurred hands grasping manically at production lines. Factories and sidewalks, arcades, bowling alleys, restaurants, newsstands—everything happening in a jittery fast-forward.

The most famous series of the movie. The Grid.

The exuberant music is employing skinnier, faster, more agile tones. It is growing more complex, the numerous voices are counterpointing each other at a strobe rate. With multiplying intersections the melodies interface ever more intricately.

If this 24-hour electric seizure is the ultimate estrangement from the nature that threw us here upon this Earth, it is nonetheless our vitality at its most potent. The city, a place with dumbfounding abundance. It is the jarring juxtapositions and impossible complexities of Thomas Pynchon's mega-novels, the nesting, proliferating pathways of accumulating audacity.

All of this exists because there are vast amounts of coal and oil in the earth.

Donna Haraway: "This is a struggle over life and death, but the boundary between science fiction and social reality is an optical illusion."

The city flowing into its channels. Chaos arranged by systems. Freeways, train stations, factory floors, revolving doors—there is a similarity to their lines and motions. This is humanity aggregated into its flows. The very gridlines of our civilization.

(I went and found time-lapse videos of beehives and anthills, because I wanted to see which species controlled its chaos with greater method. The answer was the humans, undoubtedly. We work so much more robotically than the bees or the ants. It was not even close at all.)

The music in The Grid is joyous, there are literally

human voices singing in tones of glory. Glass might have chosen something dour to remind us of the despoiled land, he might have given an icy tone to say that this place has dehumanized our spirit, but instead he chooses jubilee. He asks us to confront the fact that there is immense energy to our quotidian life. This is us. The incarnation history has chosen.

Without these cities no possibility of building the rockets that push humanity toward the stars. No airplanes to connect the world, no Internet to pool our knowledge, none of this perverse plenty.

No frenzy. No megawattage casting amber glows upon the low clouds. No all-night raves consumed by every kind of human being. None of us here together, as one, pulsing to clocks with no regard for the astral cycles.

No multiplexes, no major motion pictures and coast-to-coast distribution. No possibility of seeing humanity projected upon immense screens. No chance of pondering ourselves from unique angles.

There is nothing like these shots of a never-ending, hypertrophied highway of hot dogs spilling through a factory's metal gears. So much food consumed in a single day! It is senseless: food is produced so that it can be consumed in order to give humanity the energy to produce more food. What is it all for? I cannot help but love these tubes of surplus meat liquefied by high-pressure pistons—they are made for us, by us. For our pleasure. A modern treat. Out of all possible worlds, our collective imagination has given us the one with rivers of hot dogs. Undeniably it is ours. These hot dogs are a cord in the flow of human joy, energy, frenzy, one flow among the many that perpetuate our lifestyle, the flow of oil, the flow of missiles, the flow of traffic, the flow of money.

So much of everything. We are a mass civilization. A *mass*.

Paul Valéry: "The machine rules. . . . They want well-trained humans. . . . They are shaping humanity for their own use, almost in their own image."

And there it is, the exact center of The Grid, a currency counter rifling through thousands of hundred-dollar bills at light speed. Money. *Money!* The original premise, the hand of God that cast us out into the city, the mass delusion that makes every other mass delusion possible. If only Reggio could film it circulating. Those would be the true gridlines, the veins of civilization flowing in shapes that nobody has ever before witnessed.

At last, a point-of-view drive through the grid at high speed. The camera is moving so fast that the streetlights appear as long, strobing cords of neon. And we are getting faster yet. It's all still accelerating, the neon cords are getting longer, blazing harder, pulsing, pulsing ever more furious! A fervid scream moving toward some explosion.

And then it all stops. Silence. Barely the sound of the still air. High in the sky, straight down, the God perspective.

Alien tones of low, ponderous feedback. Music unlike any we have heard in this movie. We are looking at miniaturized grids from outer space, all of Manhattan within just a smidgen of screen. They have been colored in aquas, purples, and black. Reggio intersperses them with magnified images of microchips. The feeling is frigid, lifeless, airless.

Thomas Pynchon: "For it was now like walking among the matrices of a great digital computer . . ."

It is all a matter of scale: from up in space we are a microchip; from the clouds we are a pulsing grid; from the ceiling we are a beehive.

What are we from behind a computer screen? When seen through two eyes walking down the sidewalk? When we have been aggregated into numbers and arranged in orderly columns?

Now a crouched man in coveralls, middle-aged, his graying hair brushed cleanly back, rows of electrical dials behind him. A palette of wan greens and blues. It looks a little like he lives inside a vast machine. As he palms his forehead and takes long, lingering looks toward the ground, he drags deep into a cigarette.

Richard Klein: "[cigarettes provide] a darkly beautiful, inevitably painful pleasure that arises from some intimation of eternity."

How does humanity look when glimpsed from a mind infiltrated by eternity?

To smoke is to inhale a narcotic-like substance that improves focus and causes the brain to release chemicals alleviating pain and anxiety. It is to initiate, or prolong, or potentiate an addiction, which is to say a feedback loop: the more you consume, the more you want to consume, until you are inhaling some 40 cigarettes per day, the proverbial two packs, an industrial regimen of one every 20 waking minutes.

To smoke is to burn up a product of the earth into a cloud of smoke that enters the atmosphere. You become a personal-sized industrial plant. In goes the tobacco, tar, and papers; out comes a cloud of noxious fumes.

To smoke is to engage in a small act of self-destruction for some impossible purpose. To pervert the body for an inarticulable reason, yet one that moves billions.

To smoke is to pull yourself out from the flow of industrial time and into a moment apart from the world's rhythms.

To smoke is to witness humanity as *Koyaanisqatsi* might have it.

It is a kind of faith.

With the smoking man the scale has moved from the celestial to the individual. The next shots show a series of people deep inside the city, their motion slowed just enough to provide a defamiliarizing distance.

An aging man selling tickets to a sightseeing tour. His drawn lips. The crevasses in his cheeks and beneath his eyes. He is ignored. The exact measure of "lost in the crowd." His futility moves me.

A middle-aged office woman with a cigarette poking out from her lips, failing to raise a flame from her lighter.

A prostrate indigent being lifted off the sidewalk and onto a gurney. In one coordinated thrust he is off the ground and onto the thin white sheets.

A thick, naked man sitting in an open window. He waves his arm in a gesture of rejection, as though to avow, *who knows!*

A hand in the hospital amid a row of gurneys, a bloody IV strapped to its wrist. The fingers waggling, gripping at the air. A nurse's hand reaches down, and it clasps right on like a baby.

A young man in a beret and leather jacket, his large nose curving down over a wispy mustache. He shakes the hand of an ice cream vendor, he smacks his lips down on two scoops of pink. As his mouth closes on the cone he relishes it so much.

More than anything else in this movie, these shots have been critiqued as dehumanizing. I see it otherwise: they penetrate through the layers of meaning in which we have swathed ourselves. Not dehumanized people; rather, people stripped of the layers that have covered their humanity—the layers we often believe *are* our humanity.

The penultimate shot is the launch of a doomed rocket. Almost an exact recreation of movie's second shot, the Saturn V launching off the Earth's surface and to the moon. The same tight framing, the same magnificent pillar of fire erupting, the same uncanny movement upward.

But this rocket is doomed.

It hurtles upward into the blue heavens.

It explodes.

This portent four years before the *Challenger* fell out of the sky, killing seven.

Twenty-one years before the *Columbia* incinerated in the atmosphere, killing seven.

Twenty-nine years before the space shuttle was retired, after two of the five had ended as fires in the sky.

And still we are building pathways to the stars. We are planning towers to peak in the upper atmosphere, we are planning missions to the nearest star, we are aiming to throw humans to Mars.

Why does life never stop reaching for more?

2006, THE TRUE IMAGE

The Double Life of Véronique, Krzysztof Kieslowski (1991)

We are all the result of chaos.

No one has ever told me why my parents met. Nor why my parents' parents met. Nor what brought their ancestors to the New World and how they came to reside in New York. My parents have never given me an account of why they fell in love. Nor why, after two children and 13 years of marriage, they declared their want of a third child. I do not think they could ever explain to me why I was conceived on one night and not another. How could I ever ask such a thing, and even if I did broach the subject how could they ever say why that night and not another?

My parents had no say over which 23 chromosomes collided with which 23 chromosomes, how those 46 random pieces fitted together into a pattern of molecules that the universe will see just once. My mother had no choice in her body's decision to not spontaneously abort me, nor its decision to make me into a boy and not a girl. As I grew within her, how could she ever account for every molecule she consumed, every one of her emotions, every sight and touch and sound that registered upon her fetus? How could she know what effect Mozart would have versus Elvis, how much broccoli to consume versus how many bananas?

For less than nine months I was wrought. Why did my mother's body release me before my appointed time? How did I emerge there, tiny, premature, having already gone through so much yet barely having begun to feel the grips of what was to squeeze and bend my fiber?

So ushered onto this stage, we thirst to know what we are.

What does it mean that animate matter wants to know what it is?

Jean Baudrillard: "For if the divine mission of all things is to find their meaning, or to find a structure on which to base their meaning, they also seek, by virtue of a diabolical nostalgia, to lose themselves in appearances, in the seduction of their image."

And how was it that 17 and one-half years after I emerged I watched with my parents a movie that would alter me? And that just over 19 years after I emerged I watched a movie in a college dorm that would alter me? And that 22 and one-half years after I emerged I watched a movie with a woman I had fallen in love with that would alter us? And that almost 27 and three-quarters years after I emerged, at the beginning of a summer never to be repeated, I saw this movie that will be a part of me always?

It is correct that Kieslowski's first shot is of the twilit sky, it throws my thoughts onto the heaps of stardust that gathered to form these celestial bodies, that have also poured themselves into you and I. With the next shot we see that we have looked through the eyes of a little girl peering upside down at the heavens. Her mother explains: we know it's Christmas Eve because we can see that star.

I think this twilit sky is the little girl's first memory.

A single oboe plays a mysterious symphony's theme. We will hear this music again and again. It is extraordinary. Were I permitted to make whole just one of all the world's unfinished music, I would have no hesitation. I would give us this.

A little girl clutches a leaf before her gaping mouth. It is the first leaf of spring. A magnifying glass makes her eye gigantic. Her mother explains that we know the spring is coming because this little bit of green has appeared on those empty branches.

The eve of winter, the eve of spring. A Polish mother for the winter, a French mother for the spring. Death, rebirth. So effortlessly has this film staked its ground.

Kieslowski has been purposeful in placing mothers into these distant memories, because when we catch up with the girls as young women, the mothers are dead. These small memories will have redounded through their lives.

Kieslowski: "The main theme of this film is 'live more carefully.' Because you don't know what the consequences of your actions may be. There are people around you whose lives and well-being depend on your actions."

The opening credits are set to choral music like budding tulips. As the names flash, Kieslowski projects Weronika, no longer a toddler peering at the stars, now a woman in her early twenties. It is the movie's most pivotal scene. In Kraków's central square someone bumps her headlong. She drops her papers, she stares in a daze, she stoops to recover them. This action blurred and shadowed, as though a dream fading in the morning sun.

And now Weronika is singing the cheerful choral music amid a choir of schoolgirls beneath a late fall sun. She is snow that nobody has yet stepped in and never will. I'd never buy a white silk shirt as perfect as Weronika, because I would only ever think of that first speck of grime. But she will never grime. Kieslowski has seen to it. She will be this perfect forever.

As the chorus sings, hers is the most beautiful voice, the most angelic face, the most graceful smile, her eyes within beatitudes.

From time to time film has given me Weronika's eyes. Film has transported me deepest into that stare, deeper than music, than the written word, than the canvases of Rothko, than the great slabs of desert stone that have made my eyes flush with eternity. Still none but film have so forced my knees before the mystery. I see so much of the mystery here, in this film about Weronika and her double. About the mystery of birth and death and rebirth, this cycle flowing through that unfinished symphony.

A rain begins to shower the choir, and as the schoolgirls flee Weronika remains, singing until she is the only one left there, the only one carrying the music. If anything the drops gild the sounds ringing from her body. She holds one final, gleeful note, some last music exiting her most beautiful lips and weaving between the drops, the note goes on and on and on. Such utter splendor. Weronika is pristine youth, the wholeness of an egg without a crack.

The schoolgirls laugh and dash through the rain, they make petite leaps around a loud truck hauling away a statue of some long-dead apparatchik.

Now we meet Antek. It is nighttime. Weronika's inviting body is pressed against a green wall, a wall so full with green, the whole shot green-filtered, this gorgeous woman's hair and her white Catholic shirt are wet and matted against her flesh, an angel's smile is on her face, her long legs are clamped onto Antek's hips, the rain shimmers around them. Such ravenous hunger. Such youth. Abandon, an abandon that can only be felt by those who must satiate a life-long starvation. Who *must*. A thing those lips have needed for so long. This is the condition of our first embrace. No boredom yet, no consequence, no routine. All of that will come with age, but for now our only purpose is to end this starvation.

It is glorious how Kieslowski has cleansed this encounter of any context. He makes it elemental, just two heaving chests, an empty streetcorner. And here I believe I discern Kieslowski saying, look, this is who we were in Poland as they hauled away the statues. A people seduced. A people speechless with revolution. A people who felt new. One world succumbing to another, for a time those communal fires bringing everyone back to youth.

Weronika is this newness, her beauty is a purely cinematic, complete purity. I admire that film can distill reality, and so seduce me into believing in a purified life where it is possible for a young woman to lie naked in bed and feel the tongue of her lover against her thighs, no errors, no awkwardness, her perfectly lit body stunning as she stares up at a flawless black-and-white photo of her unblemished smile, while the haunting theme to a beautiful symphony plays and her eyes take on a trance-like quality.

Weronika is even perfect in her pains. She awakes from a deep sleep with the most girlish squeal. As the agony seizes her chest, she bites down on her hand so fetchingly.

She decides to be with her aunt, and so she leaves Antek without a word. And it is here, in Kraków, her aunt's city, that it all will happen. But not just yet. On the train she pulls from her purse a small, clear plastic ball with three stars in it. Weronika places her eyes behind this ball and stares into the plastic, seeing within it the world turned upside down. The steeple of a church bends downward.

This hidden world projected through the ball, is it not a metaphor for the act of film? Is it not a metonym of the camera that sat on the train filming Irene Jacob as she rolled through Poland, this camera encoding a second world onto strips of plastic, millions of tiny silver crystals receiving their own version of her light, the light of everything around her, this light that we all can now watch?

I share Weronika's fascination with the curved light that promises to show us an invisible world. This is the optimism of all Kieslowski's major work, this trust in the mysteries that bend our paths. Not very long ago we had just one name for this mystery, we called it God, but now there are so many godlike forces in our world: science, media, the market, psychology, technology, politics, memory, theory, law. So many adjacent realities. Human methods for drawing sense upon disorder. Film is a major one, perhaps *the* major one for us. How many times has it been said that the cineplexes are our civilization's cathedrals? Are these enormous, perfected, glamorized faces not heroes appropriate to a technologically learned humanity?

Perhaps you will disagree. Fine. *I* have seen the gods in film. My first encounter with Kieslowski's *Véronique* was late in the spring of 2006, when my life was beginning to cleave to a new reality. It felt very much like a single-serving revolution, the last fusillade of a youth that was succumbing to maturity. I had decided to put everything behind me, to change my course entirely. I was leaving, leaping: new country, new things, new identity. For the first time in years so many possibilities were open. An invigorating, terrifying summer separated me from this future. I grew accustomed to encouraging myself with some words that intruded one night; I knew almost nothing of Rilke, but they became my command: "for here there is no place that does not see you. You must change your life." So I told myself, again and again, "you must change your life." And then soon after I had learned to say those words, *Véronique* capped me like a bolt. Yes, I thought, there *is* no place that does not see me. I must live up to it. *I must.*

I could see the analogous lives creeping alongside me. I understood that though the human consciousness is limited to just one life at a time, art can be plural, and film most plural of all. It can orchestrate multiple realities into a single story. Kieslowski does not trade in cheap devices, he gives no literal demonstrations that crush mystery. He seduces. He showed me just a few days in the lives of two women who are jostled by the invisible all around them, and suddenly I knew that my life was not alone.

At her aunt's home Weronika sees the healthy, middle-aged woman with her lawyer. I have to settle my affairs, she says. Everyone in our family died while in good health.

Next she is at her friend's choir rehearsal. There can be no doubt that when Weronika begins to sing from across the chamber it is from simple joy. She has no desire to humiliate these men straining to wrest some beauty from their throats. There's no need to make their voices tin. She just can't help that music rolling through her chest.

The choir leader knows: it's been some time since a girl like Weronika sang in her chambers. She invites her to audition for the lead in a choral symphony, and although the young woman is a complete outsider, not even trained for voice, there is no question of her victory.

As she strides through Kraków's central square with an oversized portfolio that bears the music she will transform into currents of air, a headlong streak smacks it from her hands. Dazed, she stares. Wind scatters the papers as she rushes to reclaim them. There are shouts all around Weronika, scattering mobs, a roaring police truck, lines of helmets and shields. In the chaos of the shifting order she struggles to pick back up her papers.

It is absolutely correct that this most pivotal scene takes place amid revolution. *Véronique* is a movie about the imperative to make order from disorder, these beliefs that we cling to endlessly seducing us toward new forms. This nation's struggle to topple colossi and find what order comes next—so goes the battle for self in young minds.

And here they are.

A siren blares, Weronika twists her body. In the distance some tourists scurry back into their bus. She stares. Something is there. It is her. Her double. *Her double.* As though you saw a perfect copy of yourself just a little bit beyond arm's reach. While revolution screams Weronika cannot tear her eyes from this double eagerly snapping pictures of the escalating scene, now taking lingering, backward steps into the tour bus, still capturing the brisk light as the vehicle flees the square, she is stealing one last image without realizing that it will change her life.

Roland Barthes: "The photograph is the advent of myself as other: a cunning dissociation of consciousness from identity."

All is quiet now. Walking down a city park smothered in yellow dusk, Weronika heaves her soft body onto a cement column. Hand clutched to chest, hunched, she lurches toward a bench. She is bent over in agony, gasping.

This is three times now that Kieslowski has warned us. It is coming. It is building to the moment when Weronika makes her symphonic premiere.

Kieslowski once recalled a teenager who watched *Véronique* thrice. She said it made her see that we really do possess a soul. She told the director, Your movie has made me believe in my soul. He was beside himself with pleasure. I understand this woman. *Véronique* opens every last door in my skull. It assures me that life is not the world. It endlessly brims with meaning, but not *a* meaning.

Film can alter one's relationship with reality. It can impart a sense of revelation. It is art treading upon worship's grounds.

Could any other art form instill the belief in a soul? Possibly, though I doubt it. But surely none with greater faculty than film.

Film mesmerizes, it blinds me to the world while its suggestions possess me for hours, days, their traces there for life. One despondent Friday I watched Agnès Varda's *Vagabond* and that bohemian freedom, that tawdry self-reliance has always kept with me. It showed me a new way, and with just a few frames it is all enkindled once more. Just the other day, what a hush befell me as I watched Terrence Malick's *Tree of Life*, how it freed me to talk about God and death with the woman who had sat there beside me.

Film must go to the darkest places to instill such emotions, so perhaps we can forgive Kieslowski for what he is about to do.

Across a gulf of ten years it is still so easy to feel the chills that rained upon my vertebrae as I first watched this symphony. A hush falls over the auditorium, a moment of perfect silence where the air itself seems to freeze in place, and then a single oboe plays the opening theme. We have heard this spectral music many times in the past 25 minutes. Kieslowski enters Weronika's point of view. On stage she watches as the conductor beckons this music forth, his dais covered in a green light. Now he turns toward Weronika. At her side the second vocalist sings in an ethereal voice: they are verses from Dante, our fate in the next world. A midnight chime sounds, Weronika's voice assumes command, and the music begins to pick up energy. The choir joins in behind her.

How can it be that no one ever finished writing this music?

From within Weronika's gaze we see the second vocalist look into our eyes with a mad rapture. This is what it is to be inside of this music, to be *creating* this mystery. The symphony crests a minor climax, it pauses for a moment, its overture has been played, and now this, the most important moment of Weronika's young life, it is about to begin. All eyes on her. The conductor beckons. Her voice resumes softly, it gains substance as it rises into her solo. Such power! This is music and film allied to produce the strongest effect they can summon!

The music has gained its momentum, and now there can be no doubt that we are moving toward transcendence. Weronika's hand rises to her chest, she wrenches over but continues singing from within that green light, she rights herself, the music blossoms, the full choir behind her is building toward a breathtaking climax. It is such glorious music. It continues to build, up up up, and right there on the verge—it pauses. I feel tears behind my eyes. The sounds that are about to come from Weronika's mouth will be extraordinary. Dare I say they will be an answer, some important answer? Weronika takes a breath to crown this music properly, she is about to sing these notes, and then she falls down dead.

A tracking shot flies over the heads of the astonished crowd in what can only be the vantage of the young woman's soul as it departs her most beautiful body.

A shot from the perspective of her coffin, handfuls of dirt covering the frame.

It has been 30 minutes so far. Were this movie to end at this moment, I could walk away satisfied with this tragic depiction of incandescent youth.

The next shot is of a woman's stomach pulsing in the throes of intercourse. I cannot help but think of rebirth, transubstantiation, the soul that would migrate into that abdomen were she to conceive at this moment. Has Weronika's soul come here to be with its other?

The only sounds are the wheezy breaths of the two lovers. The eyes of this scene resemble the blurred, undeveloped eyesight of a newborn, Kieslowski shooting with an orb-like lens that distorts and elongates, a bright glare dominating the right-hand side. I must ask: from whose point of view are we watching?

The heaving breaths grow faster, the woman's hand brushes up against a light bulb, she clutches the switch, the light glows. They look at one another in satiation. But then she is consumed by a sadness. "It is as though I were grieving," she tells him. She asks that she be left to brood in peace.

This second woman, Véronique, of course she looks exactly like Weronika.

John Berger: "The name Veronica, given to the woman who is said to have wiped Christ's face with her scarf as he carried the cross to Golgotha, is doubtless derived from the words *vera icona*, true image."

She drives to the apartment of her voice tutor and tells him that she must quit now. She just knows she must. This elderly man's kind face turns to confusion, then disbelief. Outrage. You have no right to waste your talent!

Intimations of demise are still in Véronique's head at work the next day. Her music class has been cancelled, the boys and girls are instead seated in a darkened auditorium for a puppet show. The theme is rebirth. Véronique's gaze passes from the marionettes to the space behind the stage, she watches the man giving force to their bodies. She sees him in reflection, and as she stares at this image she feels the first stirrings of romance. The children watch a fallen dancer leap high with renewed life, and Véronique fixates upon her creator. He concludes the rebirth with a flourish, the momentum swinging his body around and pulling his eyes right onto Véronique's.

At the moment of rebirth their eyes drink in each other's reflected image.

Kieslowski is starting his film over. He has just sacrificed a perfect, 24-year-old woman so that this perfect, 24-year-old woman will live to see her perfection fade.

Véronique travels to the countryside where she falls into the embrace of a robust, friendly carpenter. Her father. This man lost Véronique's mother some years ago, and the weight of it so clearly bears upon him. Watching him, I always feel his loss, I understand that it would be a source of sadness that you would always carry with you. Life would continue with its joys and surprises and diversions in the same measure as before, but you would now always possess this inexhaustible sadness.

What is this shadow that attaches itself to us when we lose a person we have pledged ourselves to for a *lifetime*? Perhaps it is like this thing Véronique claims she has always felt, an assurance that we are not alone and will never be alone. Presences that we collect, that become our fiber, they never do leave us, even if death or heartbreak throws us apart.

It is shortly after the scene with the father that the mysteries begin.

A strange package arrives at Véronique's apartment: an old shoelace that she throws right away.

Later she is dozing in a leather armchair when a yellow gleam plays over her body. Poised right on the border between natural and numinous, a line we are always treading with Kieslowski, this gleam brings to mind the shaft of light that impregnated the immaculate Virgin Mary. Another sign of rebirth.

As Véronique drifts awake this glow dashes off. The shot pulls back to show the whole room, the light now stationed in a window opposite Véronique. She advances across this yellowed room, past a large dressing mirror that bears within it a red world, and out the window she plainly sees a young man in the distance hoist up his mirror.

So easily does the sensation of an invisible world dissolve.

And so easily we are again made to believe: when Véronique turns back inside there is the light dancing in the corner. It draws her toward a portfolio just like the one knocked from Weronika's hands amid revolution. She kneels down to examine the music, toying with the portfolio's string precisely as we have seen Weronika do.

The shot changes: we are looking down at her. Kieslowski gives us moments to take it all in, to connect Véronique to Weronika, to see the synchrony at work, and once he is satisfied that we have seen what he wants us to see, he knocks us flat on our back: as though seized with premonition Véronique jerks her head up, she stares into the camera. It tilts in response. The realization is immediate. It's a point of view shot. I'm seeing from the point of view of that yellow light.

Which can of course only be the point of view of Weronika.

Kieslowski holds the shot of the young woman's curious gaze. What is Véronique seeing at this second?

André Breton: "I am concerned, I say, with facts . . . that present all the appearances of a signal, without our being able to say precisely which signal, and of what . . . that convince me of my error in occasionally presuming I stand at the helm alone."

This is the movie's only inexplicable scene. Every other mystery in *Véronique* has some explanation. But not this one. There is no source for the second light. There is no explanation for why Véronique looks right up into the camera.

Why does she return downstairs and fetch the shoelace from the trash?

Why did I accept those lines from Rilke as my truth?

Why did this cinematic bolt become a piece of my destiny?

Baudrillard: "Only signs without referents, empty, senseless, absurd and elliptical signs, absorb us."

Véronique washes off the shoestring, blowdries it, takes it to her desk. She unrolls her electrocardiogram and draws the fiber over it. It hangs suspended just above the paper in a limp curve, and then in one violent gesture she pulls it taut.

Flatline. This thing that makes us adults, it has so often absorbed Véronique's attention in the few days we've known her. She has seen the weight it puts behind her father's eyes, she has seen the schoolchildren unnerved by the death of the puppet, she has felt the fact of her own demise. And now she has seen *something* this day.

She is also in love, really, truly in love with that puppeteer. When she visited her father, she told him *I can feel it, I have found my life's one true love.*

The shoelace is a plot from one of the puppeteer's children's stories. Véronique reads it. She reads others. He sends her more items from these tales. She comes to look upon the mailman with an expectant eye. It is a classic seduction. The girlish laugh as her slender fingers turn his pages, the crisp way her wrists wrench open his mail—so is their incipient romance nurtured.

But is this love? Little clues and games that create a private economy of signs. Quickening divertissements. What do tiny charms that ignite a young woman's fancy have to do with love? What are they compared to that thing that has always connected Véronique and Weronika? We speak the word *soulmate*, we use the term *my other half*, and we are drawing upon ancient ideas that there was once an original, androgynous soul. This hermaphrodite split into male and female halves, and love is when these two pieces rediscover one another. Is this really what Véronique feels for Alexandre? Or rather, isn't this what Véronique feels for Weronika? That trust that someone has always been with you, that irreconcilable sadness when Weronika dies. Not an androgynous original, an original that was doubly female, a body that is its own other, that always knew it was also over there, a body that is plural.

Slavoj Žižek: "So in *The Double Life of Véronique*, perhaps, we are not dealing with the 'mystery' of the communication between two Véroniques but with one and the same Véronique."

At last an audiocassette arrives. It brings the following sounds to Véronique's ears: someone exiting a house and driving in a car; steps though a busy train station; a waitress clearing a table at the station's café; an explosion. Another mystery, another seduction. Véronique sees that the package was mailed from Gare Saint-Lazare, and early next morning she sets out there. As she walks down the road she passes the burned husk of a car. She finds a café in the station. The waitress's voice rings out exactly as on the tape. There is an empty table with a pair of eyeglasses, several audiocassettes, a tape recorder. A package has been readied for the mail. Shyly, Véronique sits down. Behind her appears Alexandre, who then takes his seat across from her.

I feel the insufficiency of words. There is no way that a block of text can recreate the nest of visual and audio signals that Kieslowski spins together in the minutes Véronique rushes through Paris toward Alexandre—the female visage on the stamps that recalls Weronika, the carefully orchestrated landscape of greens and reds that Véronique walks through, the recurrent sounds that I recognize like breadcrumbs marking out a path, the mysterious Polish woman I glimpse in the background and recognize from Weronika's symphony, that ultimate ghostlike reflection of Véronique in the café's glass doors as she takes her final steps toward Alexandre's table, the irrational shots of the burned-out car being hauled onto a flatbed truck that keep intruding on the storyline. This series of little instants of "ahh, now I see," it is a microcosm of Kieslowski's entire film, which is a seduction, a stringing-me-toward, a masterful use of image and sound to make me see my world his way. A total success, this movie colonized my visual anatomy. My mind constantly wants to view the world through its logic. A gram of *Véronique* fills my bloodstream better than the whole of ten other movies. When I watch it I feel as though I am moving toward a part of myself that has always been waiting to be found.

But I never quite understand what Kieslowski's painstaking echo chamber persuades me to see. This revelation precedes argumentation. It simply is. It resembles what some philosophers have at times called "being," the foundation. A realm of direct experience that is prior to signs, symbols, narratives, language. Truth, perhaps. What Kieslowski occasionally captures in the looks exchanged between Véronique and her father, the sanctified gaze that emanates from Weronika's youthful eyes as she sends her column of sound into the sudden rain, the assured way the two young women declare that they have always known they are plural. This is what Kieslowski seduces me into trusting, but I cannot put it into words.

Alexandre sits down opposite Véronique, and neither knows quite what to say. At this moment romance is perfection: that longed for presence finally beside you, your gazes blend and you project your fantasies. Your other can be anything you want.

Such ease is shattered the moment one speaks. Now the truth is being negotiated. And what does Alexandre say? He tells Véronique, "I wanted to see if it was psychologically possible... whether, psychologically, a woman could be made to believe . . ."

We see Véronique's face fall.

And perhaps this is Kieslowski telling us that he, too, wanted to see if it was psychologically possible . . . whether, psychologically, a moviegoer could be made to believe . . .

And perhaps this is also our reality. A species that was unhappy with the fact that it must die wanted to see whether, psychologically, it was possible to make itself believe . . .

A tear steals down Véronique's lovely face, and she runs out of the station. Alexandre chases her through the streets of the 8th arrondissement, she hides in the vestibule of an apartment building. As she watches this befuddled man gape around and blow his nose into a gigantic handkerchief, her demeanor softens, he ceases to be the puppeteer, he is just another puppet caught up in some design.

He catches up with her in the lobby of a hotel and she cannot resist his apology. They are together in a gorgeous red room.

After they have sealed their game of seduction, they are playing with the contents of Véronique's enormous purse, it is as though she has heaved her unconscious out upon the bed. It is there that Alexandre discovers this most important photograph. The one Véronque shot that afternoon in Kraków. It is one small frame on pages of contact sheets that she has hauled around, unseen, for months. She takes the page and sees her other for the first time. It is the sequel of that moment when she wept because she could feel the death of Weronika. Now she sees her there, in the photograph, and she cannot control her emotion.

Barthes: "Photography has something to do with resurrection."

She sees what only she can see in the photograph, just as I recognize in Kieslowski's film something absolutely personal. Here, in this moment of recognition, an umbilical. Light has sat buried at the bottom of Véronique's purse, and it at last reaches her eyes. So too this light that Kieslowski has recorded, a reminder of something that I must know. She weeps. It is incomprehensible, a moment of pure being that pushes far beyond rational sense and psychology, an instant of such surplus emotion that one can only be completely swallowed by it. She loses her grip. Alexandre's solution to this distress is to shove his penis into Véronique. Kieslowski's camera remains fixed on the woman's lovely face as this rarest truth is smothered in coital pleasure.

The whole of this film is one gorgeous hymn to the feminine mystique. For who would want to be the dumbfounded, piston-like Alexandre pumping his genitals, when instead you could be this most sensitive creature brimming with the rarest emotions? Who would want to be the one organizing the seduction when you could instead be the seduced?

There is an even better way: you can become the agent of your own seduction. This is what I love about the path of the artist.

Véronique's knowledge of Weronika has been awakened. Again a shot of the steeple in Kraków inverted through the lens of the child's ball, a haunting flute playing the theme of Weronika's symphony.

Véronique comes to on a mattress in the depths of night. It is the spare room inside Alexandre's lush Parisian apartment. We enter into her point of view as she wanders these dimmed, greened corridors. At last she comes upon her beau working on a puppet. Her mouth giggles in astonishment, and he gives her that cad's gleam as he holds the doll before her eyes. It is she. But something is not right. Tension as he places her hand on the body of her miniature so as to teach her to give it life. As their four hands put the thing into uncanny motion, she glances down at a second creation, another puppet, a twin, motionless, arms spread, anguished lips and unblinking eyes pointed into the air.

Why two? she asks, and like a god he responds, because when I make them perform they are easy to break.

She may as well have asked, Why one? Why am I again your puppet?

Alexandre grasps a sheet of paper, takes a satisfied breath, and reads a story of two girls who were always twinned but never knew. They were born on Véronique's birthday. They have her beautiful brown hair and green-tinted eyes. One burns her hand on the stove, and a few days later the other pulls hers away just in time. How could she have known? Kieslowski's camera remains on Véronique's face as it is slowly covered in dismay. She walks out the room in silence.

It is Véronique's life but Alexandre has named it.

Nietzsche: "We do not believe that the truth remains true once the veil has been lifted."

The film nearly complete, Kieslowski will never tell us just what Véronique thinks of having Alexandre's narrative trussed upon her most private secret. His story is undoubtedly correct, but what is it compared to these sensations that have passed through Véronique's head for her entire life? To have something that has always resisted comprehension now be explained, to have a weight that has always pushed against your psyche removed—and into that space is fitted a machine.

Perhaps the seat occupied by the soul can be better filled by what I would call a machine. Maybe so, but it would have to be one supple enough to last a thousand years, a machine to pass a thousand transformations from place to place, era to era, eye to eye. I do not know of any such thing. What I believe in is just my truth. This map that I am forever unfurling, and that I at times catch glimpses of in these films. And I do believe that Véronique's doubled life makes my body shiver because it resonates with what I know is mine. I love Kieslowski's other movies so well, and I might have chosen some other to write about here, but only through this one do I feel I can say what I have to.

A most enigmatic movie, such a confusing conclusion. Véronique leaves Alexandre behind, she drives through the dim morning to her father's home. When she reaches the gates he is working on a carpentry project, the noise of a sander obliterating all sound around him, so we can be certain that the roar of his daughter's engine does not reach his workshop. So then why does he look up? And why does she stop at the gates of his yard in order to reach out through the car window and touch the rough bark of thick tree trunk?

Kieslowski alternates between shots of father and daughter, giving the sensation that the scene is moving toward some resolution. But there will be no resolution. For again we hear the sound of Weronika's symphony approaching its climax, the climax that we know will forever be forestalled just moments before her voice should give this music its crowning beauty.

And there, right there, right on the precipice of knowledge, with Véronique's hand extended and her father undoubtedly rushing out toward her, the music climbing in intensity, right at the threshold of understanding—of truth—the scene fades, the screen goes to black.

And indeed, all of our screens will fade, one day they will all grow black. Perhaps it will be on the precipice of knowledge, or perhaps we will have crossed that threshold.

And maybe Véronique reaches out to touch the tree because she is recalling that first spring leaf her mother bade her pick up as a little girl, the first time she felt someone else beside her. And perhaps just when Weronika was about to sing that note that she will never sing, she had a sudden flash of insight, she remembered that first time she looked out into the stars, and she also knew . . .

2008, THE STATE, THE STATE
Capturing the Friedmans, Andrew Jarecki (2003)

Ford Madox Ford drops into *The Good Soldier* with a most famous line: "This is the saddest story I have ever heard." Perhaps it was. He'd originally named it "The Saddest Story," but his publisher balked at such a title. Europe was ablaze, men were asphyxiating in trenches, it was no time for such things. So instead he chose *The Good Solider* in irony.

Good old Ford Madox Ford. Now there was a peculiar gentleman.

I read Ford's book in Argentina, and from time to time I would pause to murmur to myself, "yes, this truly is the saddest story."

And then four months later I sat in a subletted bedroom in Berkeley, California, as *Capturing the Friedmans* slouched homeward. I was aghast, motionless behind wide eyes, muttering, "no, no . . . *this* is the saddest story."

I had been gone from America for two years, and *Capturing the Friedmans* was part of my re-introduction to my home country.

Capturing the Friedmans tells us an awful thing: we can be made to believe anything. More—we will take whatever truth we must. If there is enough fear and force, our brains will open up and imbibe it like a baby bird. Tools can be used to author us, and the men with the guns and the badges have no qualms about using them.

Kafka: "That is the Law. How could there be a mistake in that?"

The other thing that *Capturing the Friedmans* tells us is what certain truths we Americans need to believe.

Poor Arnold Friedman became very well acquainted with our needs.

The film starts with a few halcyon seconds from an old Friedman family home movie. We see Arnold's three sons laughing together. Arnold is there too, as delighted as we'll ever see him. This is family bliss—everyone pleased as punch with the simple fact of being together on a sunny afternoon. This is the America we print on the postcards, the pure, distilled projection of what our national culture aspires to, right here on this grainy 8 millimeter home film.

We've all known moments like this. Everyone understands why we try to preserve them.

Subsequently we see another home video, quite different. It was shot perhaps a decade later, in 1988, and the nostalgic grain of Arnold Friedman's old 8 mm camera is replaced by a chilly VHS cassette. Arnold's middle son is up alone in his room making a video of himself. His name is David. We just saw David as a young boy in the halcyon footage, and his body has changed quite a bit. It looks a little ravaged. He is very, very lanky, he wears thick glasses; already his hairline is beginning to recede. He is perhaps 20. David speaks with such clamped rage. His clamped lips say that this film is private. Private, private, private, private, private! The words emerge like little bubbles of gas out of a syringe. He just keeps repeating that word, a little icier each time.

This movie is from him to him. Period. If you are not David Friedman, get out.

What red-blooded American isn't begging our director, Andrew Jarecki, to disrespect David's privacy?

That's what we are, after all, a nation of voyeurs. We love each other's business. I'm as American as anyone, and when someone's terribly pissed off with life and cowered into an angry little corner, I want to watch him sputter with rage.

Kōbō Abe: "As a matter of fact, in the theater or in the cinema usually those who look pay money and those who are looked at receive it. Anybody would rather look than be looked at."

And, of course, Jarecki gives us the goods: after a dramatic pause, David's face creases, tears fall, and with the full force of his fury he tells the "fucking cops" to "go fuck themselves." Over and over and over.

I have been this angry. It is a tiny chamber with unbreakable walls.

The film cuts away before we can figure out where David's rage is headed, but we soon get the gist. Poor Arnold Friedman, loving father, devoted husband, all around nebbish, pushed-over man—if you saw him on the street you would find him of no account whatsoever—Arnold Friedman is sexually attracted to little boys.

This is the '80s, which is to say, before the Internet, when perversion was much harder to sate. Back then, we all had to wait and wait and wait to fulfill our desires. There was much more anticipation in the '80s. You had to jump through more hoops to get what you wanted. You were more exposed along the way. Gratification, when it came, was a longed-for and treasured moment.

Not like now. Order a dildo and the mailman puts a hefty brown box in your trembling hands the next day. Go download a gig of porn. Arrange a hookup on Craigslist.

Arnold Friedman deals with his love of little boys by collecting dirty magazines. He has a stash and he keeps it secret from his wife and three children. But not very well. Jarecki asks poor Arnold Friedman's ex-wife, the eminently sensible Elaine Friedman, to explain these magazines to us. Elaine's a squirrely woman who weighs her words and holds grudges. It's roughly 2003 when Jarecki interviews her, which means that over the past two decades all kinds of sorrowful things have happened to Elaine. It's really been a terrible stretch, and she exclusively blames Arnold and his perversion for all of it. I mean *all* of it. But still, she still can't bring herself to utter what Arnold was doing down in his study. She tells Jarecki that he would go down there and "meditate."

The thing about Elaine, the thing we will soon learn about her, though I think we're already suspecting it at this point, the thing about Elaine is that her single greatest aspiration in life is to be middle class. She has an absolute terror of being anything but. And I do think that if you or I weren't precisely as middle class as Elaine, she would talk daggers through us to the neighbors all night long.

Somehow, good old middle class Elaine went ahead and married poor Arnold Friedman.

The thing that makes *Capturing the Friedmans* such an utterly awful film to watch is that nobody in it has healed even a tiny bit. Not even a smidgen in all this time! Their wounds are just as fresh as the day damnation descended upon them all. A terrible life, but it is also what gives this movie such grotesque force.

Is this what art requires?

I have a few cherished wounds. They are all still red and runny. I do not choose to keep them thus, and I have no foolish, false notions about the pain that bestows the gift of meaning. The simple fact is that they will not close, and after a while I took this fact to heart and I began to love them.

The last of these wounds I inflicted upon myself, and it is the worst. There may never be another, but it will suffice.

It is like an old, formidable star that I stare into at midnight.

Those of the Friedmans are swollen chest-raspberries that receive a ritual rubbing of iodine every morning. I cannot help but see that this is their identity. For, why else would you care over a thing like that so much?

Thomas Bernhard: "I was able to study what was grotesque about him. I studied the grotesqueness of his very presence, not only in connection with him and with him as a human being, but also in connection with me, in connection with everything between him and me, me and him."

We learn everything about these people through their wounds. They are nothing but living, walking, talking wounds. It is an ingenious idea: to make a film about people with the most savage and unsalvable wounds in the world.

Enough about that. Back to poor Arnold Friedman: inevitably the cops discover that one of his magazines is headed in from the Netherlands, and they entrap him. The game is up.

There are four main law enforcement personnel in this film. The first is a man who can't suppress a little smirk as he explains how he came to Arnold's front door dressed as a postal worker and delivered the illegal goods; still smirking, he says he returned an hour later and rubbed Arnold's face in the fact that he had just made the worst mistake of his life.

For all this, this first agent of the law is by far the least in love with the smell of his own shit. He seems almost a decent man. He might just view Arnold and his family as fellow human beings.

And the fact is, Arnold has a rather sick and twisted form of sexual desire, but he's no less human than you and I. We are all precisely, exactly the same amount human. This is the truth America was founded on.

With the delivery of that magazine, Arnold Friedman has sealed his fate. It is that simple. Your life really can change in an instant. What happens next is like clockwork: the cops come back with a warrant. They search Arnold Friedman's house. They find the rest of his stash.

And then they realize Arnold Friedman has been teaching computer classes to young boys in his basement.

Oh hell.

The rest of this story is like clockwork too, all the way to the last tired beat of poor Arnold Friedman's heart.

The question is precisely how many little boys Arnold

Friedman fucked in his basement. The answer the cops give is patently insane. They seem to believe that Arnold was having full-on little boy orgies every Monday, Wednesday, and Friday for years. I don't claim to know the truth about Arnold Friedman—for all I know he did touch little boys. But I do know that the cops' version of things is simply ridiculous.

They arrest Arnold Friedman while his wife is out buying a Thanksgiving turkey.

We can all readily agree that it's a terrible thing to come home from buying a Thanksgiving turkey to find your husband arrested for touching little boys, but I still can't help but hold it against Elaine that her love for Arnold clearly ends the moment some man with a badge tells her that her husband is a serial rapist. I just can't stand how her tune changes once she sees that badge. She later divorces Arnold while he's serving a life sentence, contemplating killing himself for the insurance money. After that she goes and marries some perfectly decent man and buys a home and names it something like Peace Sanctuary.

That's Elaine.

They have a photo of the look on her face when she comes home with that turkey. Andrew Jarecki shows us that photo, I would say, because this is a film about identity—what we think we are, what we know we are, what our society tells us we must be—and this photo is that instant when the whole fragile bubble of persona is trampled by men in leather with guns and badges.

They don't include this in the film, but on that night the cops also arrested Elaine Friedman because the poor woman couldn't stand it. For about fifteen minutes she completely lost her mind. She and the cops and poor Arnold Friedman and their son David—they all lost their mind a little that night.

Temporary insanity is what they call it. That moment when you are duly informed that you're actually not what you think you are.

It's only natural you'd need a bit to digest that.

I have known that span. I have known my fuzzy heart and my own stuttering breath and the cold sensation of a numbing body.

And just once, just one time in my life, I had the agony of bestowing it upon the one person I love more than anything else on earth.

The next hour. That next hour! The horrors I saw as she experienced "temporary insanity."

That was years ago. I can look at that hour now. I can look at that hour in my mind's eye and feel my heart begin to thump, the sweat begin to moisten the spots between my toes.

I can look at it, and when I do I can almost feel the terror I felt that night.

The wound that won't heal, the worst and last wound, my cold white midnight star.

George Steiner: "It is not the past that rules us—it is the image of the past."

Poor Arnold Friedman's youngest son comes home next. The men with badges and guns have big plans for him. Jesse, you see, was foolish enough to help his father teach computer classes. So of course, the logical thing to do is to assume that Jesse liked to rape little boys too. And just like clockwork Jesse is sucked into poor Arnold Friedman's living nightmare.

Next comes David. Stop for a second and just think about what he finds, instead of Elaine with her Thanksgiving turkey: (1) his father, arrested as a pedophile; (2) his brother, arrested as the same; (3) his mother raving and restrained; (4) the cops swarming his house.

The police deny him entrance to his own home, so he sticks a pair of Fruit of the Looms on his head.

What sick, sick sense. From atrocity to absurdity to farce. What comes next? What is possibly left?

This.

David is interviewed by the local media with a pair of white underwear on his head.

Of course! When civilization falls and we are all left starting fires with splintered matches in trash cans, there will still be the local media to interview the children of alleged pedophiles.

Once the police yank poor Arnold Friedman out of the holding cell where he's been smeared with his own shit and had his glasses stomped half a dozen times, once they deliver him back home and let him prepare for trial, David begins filming the disintegration of his own family.

There's a journalist who is introduced right about here. She specializes in the investigation of Arnold Friedmans, that is to say, patriarchs who have been made to play the loathsome rat to the state's fat feline, and this journalist tells us that the natural thing that good families do at this point is pull together. They all line up behind the father. They sit around at the kitchen table every single night for three years with staplers and Xerox machines. They work on the goddamned case! And when they inevitably lose the case, they get back to the staplers and the Xerox machines, and they work on the goddamned appeal.

This is their life for years.

Their father, the cockroach.

But the Friedmans have their own way of doing things. Here's the crux of the matter: Arnold and his three sons never doubt his innocence, and Elaine never doubts his guilt.

It doesn't take a genius to see that's not going to work.

Everybody who's ever been involved in a really, really bad family fight knows that after the worst has past, it comes time to ironize the situation. You've all driven each other to tears, but you're a family, you love one another, and you have to find some way to keep together. So, just to let your guard down a tiny bit, just to show your mother that you really do still love her, you make a small joke. It's the only way to get across the impasse and begin talking again like normal human beings.

The Friedmans get to a point where even irony fails.

They do try the jokes, but the jokes don't work. They are pitiful and flat, and no one gives them the least notice. The

Friedmans walk along an infinitely knotted little Möbius strip in full knowledge that there is no end in sight. It is mechanistic. They have been dehumanized by the brutality of a trial they know cannot be won.

László Krasznahorkai: "The meanings of words had faded like the light in a worn-down flashlight."

These are what we see on David's videos. This mechanistic facsimile of family life. His adolescence.

The videos reach their nadir with Jesse's last night of freedom. The brothers rip with laughter until the first rays of dawn. Manically. As though they were from Goya. Eyes wide, teeth ajar, ravenous for laughter. What else would you do? Your brother, convicted of the most unspeakable crime, upon the most questionable evidence. They have already cried at the system of justice that is destroying their family. They have already raged against the loss of everything good in their life. And now, impotent, torn asunder, dashed to the winds, what else can they do but laugh?

Andrew Jarecki records an interview with one of the prosecution's key witnesses. It's about 15 years since trial, and I will not call this poor creature a liar. It's quite clear that he needs to believe what he tells Jarecki. These things! Arnold Friedman had us drink orange juice laced with his own cum. Arnold Friedman said whoever drank the most didn't get raped that day. He fidgets uncontrollably. His voice wavers with each memory.

And then, out of nowhere, a tirade about his father, whom he makes sound like a far bigger scoundrel than poor Arnold Friedman ever was, and he even goes so far as to say he liked being molested by Arnold because it made him feel like he had a father.

Imagine, your whole adult identity plugged into you by some cop dying to prosecute Arnold Friedman.

Heidegger: "There is no crime without law."

There are other students that Jarecki interviews, students who find the whole thing mad. People point out that students who alleged several sex crimes per class—heaps of sex crimes for weeks on end—these children re-enrolled for the very next session.

No one ever came home bruised.

No little boy ever pulled his father aside.

No one ever woke up screaming in the depth of night.

No one said a single thing until the cops decided poor Arnold Friedman was a serial rapist.

During the trial the Friedmans decide that Arnold is a rock around his son's neck, so the ever-so-upright lawyer-at-law Peter Panaro advises them to turn Arnold loose. They go off into a jury room to discuss this.

A bailiff tells Jarecki he heard screams from that room.

Arnold throws a chair against the wall.

I've always remembered this moment because it's the first of exactly two times that I see poor Arnold Friedman show any bit of personal will. Throughout this entire movie he just sighs, casts his eyes downward, and evades. That is it. Arnold, the fulcrum around which this entire demented tragedy turns, he's but a shadow with the weakest will possible.

And then he puts a chair into a wall. It's not a whole lot, but at least now we know there are some things that even Arnold Friedman will not tolerate.

It's monstrous how you see the hairlines recede in this film. The film's morality is all in the hairlines.

Arnold: you can see his hair has long since withdrawn over the crown of his head to a cranial outpost from which it will send out little wavy scraggles for the sake of decency. Whatever got it there is long since over, and now that hair isn't moving a single millimeter one way or the other.

Jesse: as a young man standing trial his hair is beautiful, resplendent. The hair of the careless boy! After prison there's a pathetic little mustache atop his forehead, surrounded by an oval of skin. What remains on the sides is thin and untended.

David: his hair is parted in a crook far back on the left side. The hair in the middle is going so quickly it almost looks like a combover. It is hair of an adult resigned to a long life.

Upright Friedman attorney Peter Panaro: good hair, trim and confident. Peter Panaro may live to be 100 years old but he will never lose another one of those bristly beauties!

Lead detective Frances Galasso: short, well-sprayed hair, almost butch. This is hair that tells any enterprising male that he better damn well know what he's fucking getting into.

Child-interrogator Anthony Sgeuglia: his hair is gunmetal gray, hasn't receded much at all. It is pushed back like a mobster, segmented into thick strands with heavy doses of gel.

So how does it all end? Arnold, who has maintained his innocence since day one, against whom there is no evidence but the testimony of his students, cops a plea to save his son. Years later he wraps a cord around his neck in a prison cell, thereby rendering unto his children some $250,000.

Willful act number two.

Jesse, whom they seem to have convinced will be saved if his father perish, agrees to not only cop a plea but to also tell the court that his own father molested him.

For that he gets 13 years, the maximum sentence allowed by law.

The judge admits for all the world to know that she never had any doubt about Jesse's guilt, even before she saw a single piece of evidence.

And why not?

Really: why not?

This is America after all, where we know certain truths to be self-evident. And we will stop at nothing to prove them to whoever dare doubt what *the fuck* we believe. You will know these beliefs. You will know our justice—just wait. You will know the lengths we will go to in order to obtain it. And if you don't like it? If you don't want our justice?

There are people you can ask about that.

I think it's possible that at some point in his life Arnold Friedman raped at least one little boy. A crime, undoubtedly. A disgusting crime. The very worst crime I can imagine. Under our standards of justice and morality it is more than acceptable to punish Arnold Friedman for this.

Seeing poor Arnold Friedman punished for breaking the law is not what disturbs me about this heinous story. Not at all. What horrifies me is the way the state wields its power upon its helpless subjects. The way it all moves along slickened rails without the smallest doubt. The look that enters those cops' eyes every time they talk about child molestation. The pliers and needles they wield in the professional pursuit of justice. The fact that justice is never simply justice, it is justice plus violence, justice plus gloating, justice plus sanctimony, justice plus obsession, justice plus compulsion.

The way they destroy all the Friedman brains as surely as if they jabbed an icepick past their eyeballs.

They way they annihilate five people who never stood a chance.

It was all so easy.

Like clockwork.

Another day in the office.

The way I just said it to her.

That thing I *had* to say.

That thing I *had* to say so badly that I forced aside all doubts, all compassion, all morality.

And just did it.

Temporary insanity.

I wonder what harm I caused. I can never ask, even though it's all been ironed out. Even though we talk every day and share smiles and kisses and embraces. I can never ask and she can never tell. There are some parts of the mind not available to us. Not to me or to her, just there, locked deep, radiating who knows what into your life.

And so I stare into my cold white midnight star.

Stanley Cavell: "The world *is* silent to us; the silence is merely forever broken."

Jesse spends his entire twenties behind bars. When he finally becomes free again, he does two things.

Number one: he fights like hell to clear his name.

Number two: he goes to see his mother.

Somehow Jarecki manages to film Elaine Friedman moments before she is reunited with her son Jesse, after thirteen years in prison for the crime of child molestation. We see Elaine awash in trembles.

Jesse knocks.

The way she murmurs "oh shit" just before seeing her son for the first time since he went to jail.

Their wounds are all still bleeding.

2009, MAN IS BORN OF WOMAN
3 Women, Robert Altman (1977)

I was about to be 30.

At dusk I jogged up a dirt path into the foothills. It was a long, demanding climb, the struggle cleansed the static from my head. My eyebrows filled with sweat. As my legs bit into the steep a satisfying burn radiated through my calves. With each deep breath I felt more and more distilled. I was just these beats, this body, entranced, a conduit for the flow of blood and inspiration. From nowhere I spoke. Childhood is over. Get to work.

I meant *write*. Write every day. Write for hours.

In the sweaty foothills it was all very simple. You must write, go write. Yes, yes, of course. But back down below, stilled, showered, softened, once again enveloped in the clamorous everyday, it was not so clear.

In order to become what one must it is necessary to instill a practice. We practice and practice and practice, and slowly our world is filled with the manifestations of a new habit, a new identity. Thus a brain changes a brain. We must occupy our role until it is as habit.

Habit, the banks of the river of self.

Several months later I saw a young woman in a soft pink dress who looked and behaved like a child. I watched her walk beneath the moonlight late one night, lost within herself, somehow her body now perched on a second-floor guardrail high above a swimming pool. As she looked down at her reflection in that blue water I could hear the lotus melody of an oboe.

Robert Altman: "Gerald Busby's music for *3 Women* is so perfect I don't know how to talk about it.

It really is that perfect. This quiet, ominous music, it is some of my favorite of all movie music. It is the first thing we hear as Altman's camera pans slowly over a mysterious woman covering the bottom of a swimming pool with a mural. Her motion is languid. There is something heavy about her. She wears a large, masculine hat and a billowing bohemian dress. Her painting is a maze of impossible complexity, beside this labyrinth four impassioned, androgynous figures. They look to be caught up in a war, or an orgy.

The camera pushes into the mural until we only see fuzzy blue, and when it pulls back we are looking at the healing waters of a clinic.

There are two pairs of legs in close focus: one old and sagging, the other young and taut. Both are female. These limbs follow their meandering path through the steamy waters, the oboe makes its lotus notes.

The shot jumps back to reveal senile bodies conducted around the waters by young women. In an adjacent room, staring fixedly through a pane of glass, another woman. She looks to be a child.

This new girl, Pinkie, she was played by a 26-year-old Sissy Spacek. Twenty-six. In this movie she could pass for half that. And Shelley Duvall, who plays her foil, Millie, she was also 26. But *she* could pass for 36.

This seems Altman's point. People mature at different rates. Of the two sexes, women are the more malleable: a little make-up, arousing clothes, a penetrating gaze, and you're suddenly mature. Remove all that and you're a child. For a good chunk of your life your age can fluctuate severely.

Pinkie is completely timid and innocent, just some skinny flesh and a soft, thin dress. She goofs like a kid. She stares in amazement. And yet all the women of the clinic treat her as an adult. The effect is uncanny, as though I can see something everyone else can't. Should I regard Pinkie as the child she looks and behaves, or as the woman everyone believes her? It is confusing, and I think this is our world. We have our opinions about the people around us, but who are they when we can't see them? What would they become if we could look from impossible angles?

Millie is assigned to show Pinkie the ropes around the clinic. Pinkie immediately imprints on her, all but openly begging her to be best friends. But Millie seems absolutely oblivious. In fact, Millie seems absolutely oblivious to all social cues.

Millie is one of the stranger creations of American cinema. I regard her as being somewhere on the spectrum. She constantly drones at the people around her, always in an affectless, Valium-sedate tone, always relating an unending string of trite details from her life. She never once notices that no one ever listens. Entire conversations occur right in front of Millie while she goes on about her latest Cool Whip recipe. It's bizarre and a little sad. Even though I don't terribly like Millie, I do feel a profound sympathy for her. She just doesn't get it. She's as simple and transparent as can be, just gormless and present, not an ounce of guile, unaware that the only time someone pays her attention it's to lob an insult.

Pinkie imprints on this woman. She watches Millie with fixed eyes. When Millie is assigned to train her, she makes no effort to hide her joy.

Millie towers over Pinkie like a mother as they dress her in pool gear. She tells Pinkie to pretend she's a client, and the young woman scrunches up her eyes and leans forward with her palm in the small of her back. "Oh, mah back, mah back," she says with her Texas drawl. "Mah legs, mah legs." She loves this! She hams it up and flashes complicit, joyful smiles. She is coming on very strong. So strong it's unnatural.

As the two women practice, the moment is punctured by the first of many discordant moments that give *3 Women* a particular feel. Altman's camera suddenly zooms past Millie and

Pinkie to dart in on two young nurses exchanging practiced whispers behind them. They are identical twins, and their gossip is so tight it's disquieting. I feel the chill of intriguing mouths speaking my innermost secrets. The oboe plays its lotus notes. Pinkie too can feel this frost, and it throws her from her childish bliss. But Millie is obtuse: "What's the matter, haven't you ever seen twins before?"

Maybe Pinkie hasn't. Everything seems so new to her.

We're never enlightened as to the story behind the twins, why one character later warns, "We don't like the twins. You'll learn about them soon enough." It's just one of those odd Altman moments, just a little bit of implication and suspicion to keep us all off balance. This happens again and again throughout *3 Women*. I always want to look over my shoulder as I watch this movie. I am a Pavlovian creature for Altman to rig up.

Kierkegaard: "The purpose of asking a question may be twofold. One may ask a question for the purpose of obtaining an answer . . . or one may ask a question, not in the interest of obtaining an answer, but to suck out the apparent content with a question and leave only an emptiness remaining."

As Millie shows Pinkie the hot baths, the boss doctor and his head nurse stride up—and suddenly it is the nuclear family. The doctor is a handsome man with bushy black hair, the nurse a severe woman with a matron's coif. They surround the young on either side. Altman has shot it so that the doctor looms a full head above Millie, and he entirely dwarfs Pinkie. The nurse is slightly shorter, but still commanding. Pinkie and Millie stand in between with wide eyes upturned, mouths agape, looking like nothing so much as bad children under reprimand.

I cannot doubt that Altman means to foreground the family unit, because Pinkie and Millie have no family—no one in this movie seems to have any family. They are orphans, seemingly adrift from all familial connections. But in spite of that they cannot prevent family dynamics from steering their relationships.

3 Women is a resolutely psychological movie, and here is the first law of psychology: you cannot escape your parents. Perhaps you would assume that Millie and Pinkie have left their parents far behind, but it's clear that powerful parental demons still lurk in these minds. Altman endlessly throws us back toward images of the family, family archetypes, familial dynamics. For instance, the way Pinkie clings to Millie, she so badly wants a big sister, a mother. And now this scene, where they're being punished like children. And many, many more to come. Just wait until we meet Willie.

I can relate to these women. I too know what it is to look for family figures in adulthood. I will admit that, much like Pinkie and Millie, my parental instruction as regards socialization was meager. For most of my first three decades I was oblivious to social cues that most would take for granted. Unaware, I good-naturedly said and did things beyond the norm. Literature was the first place that I began to learn all the facts of being human that were never taught to me. I learned to see my actions through the eyes of others. Little by little I found unprecedented new insight into my identity.

Barthes: "To interpret a text is not to give it a (more or less justified, more or less free) meaning, but on the contrary to appreciate what *plural* constitutes it."

I wonder very much about Millie's childhood, for the fact is she's crushingly single, and she's endlessly striving—with total failure—to attract the attentions of men. So much effort, and still an entirely blank social life. Millie likes to have her lunch in the hospital cafeteria next door to the clinic, and there she takes lunges at the hunky interns seated around the table. She's like a shoddy knock off of a luxury brand: on the surface Millie has all the trappings of a desirable woman, but something's off. Her hair and makeup are impeccable. She goes on about the nice pool in her apartment complex, how she would just love to cook some man a delicious dinner. She both chews gum *and* smokes a cigarette—simultaneously. She even asks an intern to feel her tender throat. It's like she has read a book on seduction and is doing every last thing on the list—all at once, and *as conspicuously as possible*. But she's not getting the slightest modicum of interest. To the contrary, you can sense the clear disdain. And I get it, because I don't find Millie attractive, either. In theory I should; everything one needs for a seductive, desirable woman is right there. But it just doesn't add up. Altman is practically begging me to consider why this statuesque movie star exudes the character of a mannequin. What is it about Millie? Why *is* she so inert? She reads women's magazines from start to finish, she diligently records their recipes. She buys beautiful clothes from Neiman Marcus catalogs. Her lovely figure suits them perfectly. She even drives a feminine little hatchback in whose door she invariably catches her skirt. Yes, every single time we see her driving this car her skirt is caught in the door. Every single time! But she just radiates no real femininity.

Something must be said about Millie's two enormous front teeth, which are mated to enormous, egg-shaped eyes that always look smothered beneath their heavy lids. Millie's lips never quite close over those two teeth. The enamel continually pokes out, making the poor woman look just a little bit idiotic. I have to give it to Shelly Duvall, I don't know where she found this expression but it's the perfect touch. It must have taken some practice. It is not normal for teeth to bulge out like that. And those lazy, half-mast eyes. I can't imagine where she thought it up, how she managed to perfect Millie's constant expression. This face, it is the crown to Millie's sexless edifice.

Pinkie is not sexless. She is cute. She is one of those young women that everyone knows will be stunning one day. At the moment her body is more mature than her demeanor. Without realizing it she's turning on the men left and right. So innocent of this conversation happening all around her, this discourse where she holds a trump card—if she ever realized she'd crimson in an instant.

Why does Pinkie feel so powerfully for odd Millie? Why is she always scheming to be in her life? Why, after just a few days at the clinic, does she manage to install herself as Millie's new roommate?

The day she moves in we meet Altman's third woman. The roommates are driving home through the Southern California desert, and it's rural and desolate, nothing but sand for miles. Millie decides to introduce Pinkie to a decrepit bar known as Dodge City, what she refers to as her main hangout. She parks in the gravel lot, they walk in through the dust, and Millie points Pinkie through the back window. In the distance young men are swarming around on dirtbikes. Squatted down just beyond the back door is a witchy and very pregnant woman laboring over a lurid mural. Willie. She pins them with her two kohl eyes.

Willie moves like the hour-hand of a clock. There is something of the ancient and the eternal about her. She doesn't speak so much as train her desolate gaze on you. Her large, rigid-brimmed hat sits atop willowy dresses, her long black hair collects about her in clumps. Even beneath the noontime desert sun she looks smothered in shadows. I gather Willie is just a few years older than Millie, but she seems hieroglyphic.

As Willie strides in and serves beers, Pinkie fixes her with an enormous stare.

There's a little witch in Willie's bar, and when Pinkie pulls its string it spits on her and rumbles with a deep, echoing laugh. It's another one of those creepy Altman moments—for just an instant everything in the movie stops, and all attention is centered on that baritone laugh that goes on and on. I want to look over my shoulder again.

Millie, Pinkie, and Willie. What to make of them? Hitchcock once split his villain into three characters; the complexity of this evildoer just wouldn't fit in one person. So he doled it out among three.

And Altman splits the subject of *3 Women* into Millie, Pinkie, and Willie. What is the thing that these women add up to? Hard to say. It's swift and loose, something whose names are multiple yet always insufficient. I imagine if Altman could have said it so simply he wouldn't have made the film. Clumsily we might call it "eros's endless agon."

On their way out, Pinkie and Millie run into Edgar—the man that somehow temps these three women. Muttonchops, puffed out chest, big old ten-gallon hat. All bluff and boast, a child in a dad's body. Edgar. A question that Altman never convincingly addresses—indeed that he does not even bring up, much less address—but a question that *must* be asked, is why Willie has bothered to marry Edgar. For Willie absolutely smolders with a smoky sex appeal, and she is an artist of extraordinary caliber. The very idea that Willie could possibly stand to cohabitate with Edgar, much less consent for him to impregnate her, is laughable. Edgar is your archetypical buffoon. He hulks around in ill-fitting shirts, ornaments himself with enormous sideburns, sports alpha male sunglasses that even David Hasselhoff in his prime could never have dreamed of pulling off. He adores yanking a shiny silver pistol from his hip, waxing it around in the air, and pointing it at women. He makes atrocious jokes. He plants fake snakes under fake rocks and then pretends to kill them as some sort of means of hitting on Millie and Pinkie.

If this were a different sort of movie, the fact that Willie married Edgar would be a huge plot hole. It would demolish the credibility. But I find it absolutely, perfectly apt to *3 Women*. Of course Willie and Edgar are together! Who else would be with him?

I've got to stop right here and observe that there are an awful lot of snakes in this movie. True, *3 Women* is set in the desert, a landscape known for snakes, but it hardly explains why Altman sticks them everywhere. There are Edgar's fake snakes. There are also the ones all over Willie's art. She likes to paint the slithery creatures onto planks of wood and then shoot them full of holes and hang them around her bar. She also puts them all over her murals. The one she was working on in the back of Dodge City features a bunch of simian-looking figures staring up in enraged worship at a triple-snake high in the sky.

Altman trains his camera over this mural again and again. A most striking piece: three snakes coiled up in an enormous circle, their tails spiraling inward to form a labyrinth, it reminds me of that most infamous snake who gave Eve the apple. And it also recalls the moon. Eden's serpent and the lunar orb—the two most potent symbols of the curse that woman is made to bear. A curse that is very much the heart of Altman's film.

When the women arrive at Millie's apartment, a certain fact becomes unavoidable: Millie really, really loves the color yellow. I mean she *really* loves it! Really! Her apartment is completely yellow. Curtains, lamps, chairs, countertop, pictureframes, candles, bedsheets. Just about everything in here is yellow. Her car is also yellow. So are almost all her clothes. At one point we even see her distinguish between shades of yellow that are invisible to the other humans around her.

It also now becomes clear that Pinkie's color is, quite naturally, pink—she wears virtually nothing but. Millie's yellow is a primary color, it is full-grown, it has a fixed identity; but Pinkie's pink is immature. It is a pale version of red. For now she wears only the palest, most delicate pink imaginable, but this will change. Soon her pink will grow up.

Altman arranges the palette of this movie so carefully. Millie's yellow, Pinkie's pink. The blue of the water, the gold of Willie's magnificent murals. The red of blood that we see exactly twice.

There is so much water in this movie, so much desert. The water is supple, it is formless, chaotic. Origin and innocence. It is present at birth, it confers life and health. The desert is brutal, obdurate, necessity. It betokens death, the debts we all must pay. The healing waters of the clinic are full of female nurses. And in the desert's dead sands the men drive their dirtbikes and fire their weapons. The water and the desert. Adolescence and senescence.

The feminine and the masculine.

The blood that renews them.

Pinkie is struck with utter delight the moment she enters Millie's apartment—the home she has always wanted—but this glee soon boils over. Things get odd. Pinkie steals Millie's diary, she reads it, and then she begins making her own entries. She copies Millie's name and Social Security information onto her pay slip for work. She tries on Millie's clothes. In general she grabs anything she can take from Millie's personality. If she weren't so kittenish, this would look like some sort of bodysnatching. But Pinkie is innocent. She's just being a child.

I think we're all a little like Pinkie, trying to will ourselves into situations that will make us become the people we want to be.

Millie and Pinkie are roommates for a few days, and then we come to first blood. It is metaphorical blood. Millie is throwing herself a dinner party, she has bought grocery bags full of ingredients like pressurized cheese product and aerosol whipped cream. Pinkie wants to help prepare. There are some cans of shrimp cocktail, and as she strains to pry the cap off of one, it spatters all over the torso of her pink dress. She stares down at it: an enormous red gash like a sheet stained with blood. Enraged, Millie barks, an excessive, brutal response. It's out-of-character, like a mother whose daughter's first blood has brought back up some awful trauma. Perhaps Millie sees something in Pinkie that she despises in herself.

New people always carry the possibility of danger because they can make us see ourselves in ways we never before imagined. Although we are used to thinking of our identity as independent—the unique product of personal choice—it is nothing without community. Our societies are compacts based on the limitations we wish to observe in human behavior. Ways of being shiver through populations. One person borrows a hairstyle from another, and soon it's a trend. That remark an actor makes, quickly everyone is saying it. Facial expressions migrate between colleagues at work. Opinions circulate around our social networks and become our beliefs. Most of the time, if we contribute at all to our identities it is to embellish the fringes of the great social mass. What is the aether that these traits travel upon? They move through our gestures, our emotions, the clothes we choose for the occasion, the places we decide to be, the verdicts we level at one another. Our mores, ethics, values, aspirations, fears, doings, beings—they are gleaned from our society.

While Pinkie stands confused in her red-gashed, pink dress, Millie dons seductive garb and leaves in a fury. Pinkie pleads forgiveness, she begs. But Millie has no interest in spending the night with another woman. She wants a man. So she stalks out; some hours later she returns bearing Edgar. A married man and an expecting father, and also an oaf whom any woman can seduce, even Millie. As they trot drunkenly toward the bedroom, it is plain to see Pinkie's dismay. Her image of Millie has been shattered. It is a primal moment, that instant when the child realizes her parents are not infallible. They may not even be good people.

Eyes glistening, Pinkie clings. Don't do this! Millie's response—her unleashed fury—comes in a scream: *"Get out of my home! Go away! I can't stand you!"*

Pinkie walks out into the night. Thrown from her home, thrown from her only friend, barely dressed, without even a place to sit and dry her tears. Poor little Pinkie. Abused, abandoned, alone. This film's most desolate moment.

And now the snake begins to consume its tail. Here is the shot that all of these intimations, all of Altman's carefully arranged colors, gestures, and images have been building up to. All the many mirror reflections that have been transposing the bodies of Pinkie and Millie into one another. There are so many mirrors in this movie! Altman does things with mirrors that I've never seen done in film, implying continuity between minds, transferences, deep, divided psyches. Are Millie and Pinkie really one? Who, exactly, is Pinkie? Who is Millie? Is everything I've been watching a lie, or perhaps just one version of a truth that requires so many more angles than the one at which Altman's camera sees?

Pinkie limps along the second floor catwalk. As she leans on the guardrail the moonlight reflects off the pool's trembling waters and dances around her. It recalls the sunlight bouncing off the clinic's gentle baths, except now everything is reversed: moon, not sun; rupture, not peace; isolation, not community. Illness, not health.

The camera drops down to the creepy, angry figures painted at the bottom of the blue pool. Gerald Busby's lotus notes play. The girl stares into the waters two stories below. She lifts up the hem of her nightdress and steps onto a lounge chair. She places one foot on the guardrail. The camera again drifts down. We see Pinkie's reflection in the pool's trembling waters.

This image. The first time I saw it, already certain of what would occur, I knew I would always remember it. So much this moment let me wrest from my own depths. Such shots are the reason cinema has captured the modern consciousness. The fleeting tableau that communicates like telepathy—an image that contains everything about *3 Women* that cannot be said. This entire essay is to map this image onto language.

From the movie screen fly forth apparitions that unearth the thoughts we cannot reach on our own, cinematic equivalences for the identity that language will not contain.

Serge Daney: "The eternal return of the becoming conscious of the eternal return."

Pinkie leaps. Not *her* falling through the air but her reflection . . . until—with a violent splash, image and reality merge.

The camera pulls back to show Pinkie's fallen body floating above those grotesque, screaming figures.

Had Pinkie not met Millie, had she not become invigorated by the potential for understanding, had she not felt it crushed, had she not observed Willie's brooding force, had she not stolen what she could from them—where would she have found the poise to leap so decisively?

Pinkie's fall throws her into a coma, it throws this film into fever. All this time Altman has been quietly building an implicit question. All of the weird little moments, all of the suspicions and implications, the symbols, the colors, the reflections, the creepy music. They are all incomplete utterances that have been creasing my brow and priming my lips to whisper three little words . . .

And now, when Pinkie awakens from her coma, I do not want to merely whisper. I want to exclaim! *What . . . the . . . fuuuuck?!*

There is a certain genre of film, perhaps originating with *Last Year at Marienbad*, *La Jetée*, and *Persona*, continuing up through *3 Women*, and seen contemporarily in cult movies as David Lynch's *Mulholland Drive*, Darren Aronofsky's *Pi*, and Shane Carruth's *Upstream Color*. I will call it *the wtf?! film*. They are characterized by the aggressive use of techniques native to cinema—sharp cuts, striking images, errant scenes, breakdowns in chronology and causation, unnatural timeflows, a chaos of implication and coincidence. These are cinema's most willful attempts to speak truths only it can utter. They are perhaps when film is most purely itself, not simply telling stories but telling *its* stories. The stories film as a medium was meant to tell.

Alain Robbe-Grillet: "The spectator will let himself be carried along by the extraordinary images in front of him, by the actors' voices, by the soundtrack, by the music, by the rhythms of the cutting, by the passion of the characters . . . and to this spectator the film will seem the 'easiest' he has ever seen: a film addressed exclusively to his sensibility, to his faculties of sight, hearing, feeling. The story will seem the most realistic, the truest, the one that best corresponds to his daily emotional life, as soon as he agrees to abandon ready-made ideas, psychological analysis, more or less clumsy systems of interpretation which machine-made fiction or films grind out for him *ad nauseam*, and which are the worst kinds of abstractions."

In the 50 minutes that follow Pinkie's emergence from her coma, *3 Women* incontrovertibly becomes a wtf?! film. It forces us to doubt everything we have just seen. It moves in completely unexpected directions. It leaves a curious expression upon my face.

Millie has delivered news of Pinkie's coma to the girl's parents, and they arrive from Texas in a Greyhound bus. They are docile, bewildered, timid; most of all they are very, very old. So old that their personal identities have all but been erased by the infirmities of age.

When Pinkie awakens to find this frail woman and man peering at her in bed, she flies into a fury. WHO ARE THESE PEOPLE? she demands. Get them OUT of my room!

This can only be a shock. Pinkie has not gotten within a mile of demanding a single thing this entire film. To the contrary, she has been a model of meekness and compliance. And now, newly emerged from a life-threatening coma, still fragile, weary— in this state she fills with aggression and ejects two tired elderly people—who claim to be her parents!—she throws them out of her hospital room.

That is not all. Far from it. Pinkie paints her toenails bright red. She smokes with a seductive hand. She flips her hair and speaks quickly and wantonly. She manipulates Millie into giving her sole ownership of the bedroom. She even casually insinuates that her doctor may have raped her while she lay in coma. She lies handily, steals Millie's car, wears bloody pink, cavorts with grinning Edgar and fires his lead bullets.

It is sex, plain and simple. The desire to instill sexual longing, the feeling of such longing between one's own legs. The girlish femininity that existed before Pinky's fall has become a womanhood flush with erotic agon.

Ever since we first saw her, Pinkie has quietly absorbed Millie and Willie, and in the chaos of coma those traits have seized her mind. This is precisely what happens, is it not, as the older generation raises up the younger, only far more gradually. Parents deposit their youthful selves into their children, their own identities giving way to the dictates of middle life. In the rite of adolescence this process becomes violent. Parents see themselves as though resurrected, again fresh with hope and energy. So it is that while Pinkie struts and shoots with Edgar, Altman pointedly turns his lens on Willie, passed out at the bottom of an empty pool. Pinkie leeches her, just as she leeches Millie's home, her car, her dreams. She takes these dreams and makes them flesh.

Thus go the generations, like a snake consuming its tail.

Pinkie is staring down the barrel of her pistol and firing. The boys are falling over in bunches. Millie is scared to death and Willie is passed out on her painted tiles. This motion seems irrefutable, but then, from seemingly nowhere—all of a sudden it stops.

What brings Pinkie back to earth is a nightmare. There is no other scene nearly so spooky in the movie. Atop sinister sounds, Altman shows a mélange of shots we have already seen, plus one we have not: a man's face, his eyes and mouth covered in shadow, a hat on his head, a white shirt. He stares at Pinkie as she sleeps in her coma. All the while the witch's laughter booms. The face of this man suddenly morphs into Pinkie's father's face.

Could this be the doctor Pinkie claims stole her virginity? Is this why she disavows her parents? Is this the crux of her sudden transformation?

She dreams another shot we did not see: Edgar dancing with Willie. The Edgar she is seducing. This dream breaks off as Pinkie snaps awake. Guilt-ridden, that sleepy image of Edgar and Willie still in her mind, Pinkie wobbles from the bedroom toward sleeping Millie, begs her only friend to take her into her arms for the night.

The two women are in tears, on the brink of reconciling. This is how a drunk and lurching Edgar finds them as he lets himself into their apartment. He paws the women, makes bawdy remarks. His wife is giving birth, and he has come to play doctor.

3 Women ends with smoldering Willie pushing a stillborn boy into our world. It happens late at night in a shack behind the bar. Altman shoots it through Pinkie's awestruck gaze as she peers at two remote figures: Willie lying in bed, her feet high in the air and pressed into Millie's chest, her body seizing, her mouth screaming. In the makeshift movements of the two frantic women, it looks like some bizarre rite, some witchcraft.

And perhaps it is, for this scene tells us that woman gives birth to man. A most diabolic thing. Woman brings her oppressor into the world. Her body creates this quandary and unleashes it into the universe. She raises him and loves him. In the end he takes the world from her.

Man merely comes into this world. He does not create woman. And so for centuries he has made his lack felt; he has used his power over woman to make what is not his into something that suits his own desires.

The ouroboros. An ancient riddle that will never be solved so long as woman continues giving birth to man.

D.H. Lawrence: "And truly I was afraid, I was most afraid / But even so, honored still more / That he should seek my hospitality / From out the dark door of the secret earth."

After the storm comes the quiet. A deliveryboy brings Coca-Cola to Dodge City, and there he finds a regressed Pinkie sitting behind the counter. Not only is she regressed: there's a wild-eyed look to her, like someone who's undergone shock therapy. She wears Willie's billowy bohemian garb.

Pinkie calls to a woman that she describes as her mother. It is Millie, who is out back painting. She has never looked this way the whole film. Her lips now cover those two massive front teeth. Her eyes are sharp. Her once-flouncy hair is tight and severe. This Millie is charged with witchy Willie's smoldering looks. She is powerful and dominant.

The deliveryboy makes small talk: "Sure is horrible, what happened to ol' Edgar . . ."

Seems Edgar accidentally discharged that pistol of his into himself.

I cannot get out of my mind his horrified face as these three women gun him. Surely Edgar is a lout, a cheating, buffoonish man-child. But murder . . . ?

The delivery over, Pinkie and Millie walk out to their house behind the bar. The sunlight looks like it comes from an earlier century, as though this is not California but somewhere in the immense Midwest prairie, back when California was only a dream.

Millie and Pinkie come upon Willie. Her hair now gray, her eyes lacking their trademark kohl, she is swaddled in a pink blanket and a heavy pink housedress. A grandmother.

"I just had the most wonderful dream . . ."

In a wide landscape shot, the camera pans over from the three women's domicile, coming to rest on a pile of worn out tires.

Of all the mysterious scenes in this film, this is the most. Have the women decided to disavow men altogether, to simply live together in solidarity? What is this new matriarchy? Why does it seem to require transport to a past century?

Robert Hass: "There is something of imbalance and excess in threes."

I love everything about this film except the ending, which has always smelled unpleasantly of brainwashing, submission, Stepfordism. The interconnected lives of these three women should not become this pacified balance, just as the id, ego, and superego should never reach a tranquilized stasis. Perhaps two lovers can reach a settled state, but if there is a child, that third will keep things unbalanced. So it should be.

At no other point in *3 Women* does Altman leave me as uncertain regarding his motives. Altman the trickster, the rebellious auteur who bucked the studios at every step of his career; it is not like him at all to condone such a conclusion. So perhaps I am wrongly reading his intentions with this scene, or perhaps he means to leave me with an end as disconcerting as the lotus notes of Gerald Busby's music.

As to myself, I will choose the instabilities whose chase brings dynamism, I will have that over these calcified identities. I will nurture my habits for the stability they bring, but I will always also want the chaos that they channel. I will want that fleeting shadow that I might see at any moment from the corner of my eye and feel the entire day trip off-kilter.

2010, RE-BIRTH OF A NATION
Meek's Cutoff, Kelly Reichardt (2010)

THAT MORNING

What woke me up that morning was the sound of the telephone. It was early, and my mother was on the line. She knew better than to call me that early. Extremely courteous, she would never call before the sun had risen.

She had tried my apartment and then called my girlfriend's, where I was roused by the cordless phone's synthetic ring. My mother spoke in a panicked voice. I could not quite understand what I was hearing.

It was the end of the summer. Four months prior, my mother and father had driven seven hours to see me walk across a stage and grasp a rolled up paper meant to symbolize my college diploma. Then we had gone to Napa in the late spring heat. They bought me a gorgeous meal and filled my stomach with wines. Summer came. Three careless months reading in cafés, three months of complete freedom with the woman I had fallen in love with. Now it was September. I was unemployed. I sat there on the floor of a studio apartment, listening to my mother, who hardly ever called and most certainly not this early in the morning.

The weather was starting to turn, and I knew I'd never, ever have another summer like that again.

When I saw that third wagon topple down into the ravine at the end of *Meek's Cutoff* I thought about that end of summer, the end-of-summer drifting and the instant when life changes irrevocably, that September morning unlike any other. On the screen I saw that look of abjection on the settlers' faces, mixed with quite a bit of terror. In the time it took their wagon to shatter, their entire world was thrown into disarray, their very existence into doubt.

And then Meek, who had led them deep into the wilderness, Meek, who wasn't quite good and not quite evil either, Meek turned his ragged beard to the Native, who sat above it all like a sphinx. That look on the Native's face. Was it a smirk? Did he comprehend? Had he meant to orchestrate the wagon's long fall?

And what did he think as he saw Meek cock his gun and aim it right for his heart?

ON THE LEGITIMACY OF ILLEGITIMATE THINGS

In *The Social Contract* Rousseau tells us something so interesting that we're still puzzling it 250 years later. He tells us that good governments are formed on top of a catch-22. There must be some initial act that legitimates their rule, this being what separates a true society from a mere group of captive people. But, for obvious reasons, this legitimacy can't come from the governing class itself. Thus the catch: where does it come from? How does a government impose something on its people that, by definition, it can't impose?

There have been many answers to Rousseau's quandary. God is a good one—from the Ancient Egyptian pharaohs to the European monarchies it has a solid track record, but it's unlikely to work widely nowadays. More recently, the collective trauma of a historical calamity has done well, and this seems well-suited to the tumult of modernity. The United States has partaken in a little of this, as well as founding fathers that have been made into political deities and documents that have accrued sacramental status.

These are all functional solutions to the riddle of legitimacy, but they are not the kind Rousseau was looking for. He wanted something logical, something you could impose by dint of philosophical argument. By contrast, these other answers leverage something resembling spirituality, a collective belief that requires decades, sometimes centuries to become established. A sense of national mission, and a national narrative behind it. Such institutions are not arguable or rational. In building them, a nation must find its faith.

I wonder what Rosseau would have made of film. In the 20th century, the cinema has been of momentous service in spreading the national religion. It is well agreed that D.W. Griffith helped to invent modern America with *Birth of a Nation*, and he did so well that Sergei Eisenstein came to America to absorb the language he created, then used it to help construct Soviet Russia from the ground up. And ever since, these tools have been used with increasing force, those who would rule a nation becoming better skilled at making them instruments of indoctrination.

WATER

Seven people give up everything to settle a place they've never seen. The journey is long, the land is bleak. It is populated by humans so different from them that they find it hard to believe they're human. Their guide on this journey is Meek, a man who looks, talks, and acts like a down-on-his-luck highwayman suffering an endless hangover.

They are headed from a failing civilization to a pristine place. As Meek explains, no one knows the fate of this unsettled land. It might become part of the United States. Perhaps it will join the British Empire. Maybe it will become its own country. Or the Natives could reclaim it and kill everyone.

As *Meek's Cutoff* begins, Meek and his seven settlers are fording a river. Kelly Reichardt lingers over the shots of them moving through the chest-high, flowing water. These are slow, long takes, and often the camera is static. She shoots from far away, letting the land swallow the action, letting the tedium of the work become manifest.

The sense of transition is palpable: they are crossing out of something, and into something else. The water that forms this border is their most precious resource. They do not know how many days it will be until they next see it, so they are washing their clothes, filling their tanks, scrubbing their dishes, filling the stomachs of their animals.

When the caravan awakes the following morning, Reichardt suggests what exactly they have crossed into: Glory White's young son Jimmy is reading out loud from Genesis. God has just expelled Adam and Eve from the Garden: "And the Lord God said, Behold, the man is become as one of us, to know good and evil."

To know good and evil. Perhaps if you left civilization to be devoured by the wilderness your idea of good and evil would shift quite profoundly.

As Jimmy reads, Reichardt's camera drifts through a camp breakfast, imbuing a sense of tiny humanity walling itself together within a gigantic space. "So he drove out the man, and he placed at the east of the Garden of Eden cherubims, and a flaming sword which turned every way, to keep the way of the Tree of Life."

Have they left the Eden of civilization for a hostile and dangerous wilderness? Or is it precisely the opposite? Are they headed toward a beauty untouched by the failing political order? Meek claims that "the land you're headed for is a regular second Eden," but then again, one look at Meek and you'd doubt his every word.

These are the questions they were baptized with as they crossed into this journey unlike any other. They pulled their water from the same river, and they all bring it with them. They carry it together into this ambiguous wilderness.

THE WESTERN

The Western is the most American genre of film, full stop.

André Bazin: "The migration West is our Odyssey."

Bazin wrote that while establishing the Western as serious art. He made the big claim that Westerns constitute a modern American myth. Collectively, they tell the foundational story of the postbellum United States.

The contemporary philosopher Robert Pippin has continued Bazin's argument. He writes that the heroes of Westerns are "super-heroic, near divinities" who fight to bring civilization to chaos. "In fact, most great Westerns are in one way or another not about the opening and exploration of the frontier but about the so-called 'end of the frontier,' and that means in effect the end of the New Beginning that America had promised itself."

In other words, capitalism. The frontier might have become anything—Pippin's New Beginning—and the Western tells us, over and over to the point of propaganda, how we filled it with American capitalism. Property rights, commerce, liberal government, laws. Self-reliance. Freedom. These are the stories that the Westerns tell. The basis of the modern American identity.

Pippin notes that the great majority of Westerns take place after the Civil War—that is, after the capitalism of the North had extinguished the feudalism of the South. Hence the New Beginning. The South was in ruins. Abraham Lincoln had violated the Constitution with impunity. The United States had never come closer to dictatorship, and there was the possibility for radical change. It was what the philosopher Carl Schmitt has called a "state of exception," a revolutionary moment in which the law is suspended and anything can happen.

What happened was the North imposed capitalism on the South and colonized the West in its own image. And, decades later, Westerns legitimated these doings by telling the stories of how brave men brought the only possible civilization to a waiting continent. It is a genre of certainty, a genre of rightness. It enshrines those very American values of order, masculinity, capital, work, and freedom. Moral clarity.

Thomas Pynchon: "It is our national tragedy. We are obsessed with building labyrinths, where before there was open plain and sky. To draw ever more complex patterns on the blank sheet."

A pleasing moral clarity existed in the heyday of the Western, but since then it has been tossed into doubt. The idea of good men settling the continent for civilization has been replaced by an image of marauders spreading white supremacy. The goodness of the American project has come to be doubted. Whether because of the Vietnam War, the *coups d'état* imposed on Latin American governments, subsequent wars of aggression, or the many critiques made of American patriarchy and white nationalism, American moral clarity has dimmed.

These critiques are pervasive, and that makes the Western a tricky genre nowadays. Can you still make a Western in modern America? How would it look? What would its morals be like? How would the settlers be regarded? How would the Natives?

WORK, WAR, AND TERROR

In September of 2001 I understood very little about the world. I did not know what I wanted, and I surely hadn't learned what one must do to have what one wants. I was only just beginning to grasp how politics worked. I knew almost nothing of adult society. But even someone such as myself knew that the events of that morning would re-make my country. That was the one thing everybody knew that morning.

I sat on the floor of my girlfriend's apartment, and we hugged each other. We wondered whether these things my mother had just described were over, or if there were more of them yet to come. It was obvious that there would be a very, very severe response, and that this thing, when it happened, would be at the heart of my nation's life for a very long time. All the other debates would be cast to the side. This coming war would be the central point of public life for months, perhaps years.

Everybody knew these things on that morning.

This is what I knew: The summer of 2001 had ended. The warm days in the cafés and the careless nights were done with. I was young and unemployed, and there was about to be a recession. We were headed to war. People out there wanted us dead. Perhaps they were about to unleash more.

Work, war, and terror.

The night before, my life was still drifting. My priorities were fuzzy. Now the things on my mind were: work, war, and terror.

Work, war, and terror.

I was very far from being an adult, but I could no longer be a child.

THE LOOK OF REICHARDT'S WEST

Reichardt restricts herself to a tight palette of golden yellow, pale blue, tan, bits of white, flecks of red. I don't think it's a coincidence that Reichardt's palette is exactly the one Richard Misrach used to document the same Western America as a postmodern wilderness in the 1980s. Hers and his are dominated by over-exposed colors bleached into irreality, giving an austere, sublime, slightly plastic vision of these wilds. Misrach's West is large enough to absorb countless hydrogen bombs, and it is this emptiness into which Reichardt drops her humans.

FILM AND MYTH

It would be most unoriginal of me to argue that film is America's best maker of national myths. This has become a truism. The cinema is where we go to see our collective dreams projected skyscraper-high. No other medium has done as much to shape our morals and change the way we live.

I can tell just from watching *Meek's Cutoff* that Reichardt believes this. She tells an American story, her archetypes are American archetypes. Her film drips and breathes the Western. But she wants to craft one that is appropriate to our world. *Meek's Cutoff* means to offer a new Western story that very viscerally embodies the confusion and drift that Americans feel now, in the early 21st-century.

Unlike virtually all Westerns, *Meek's Cutoff* doesn't take place after the Civil War. It takes place in 1845, when the Civil War was a foreboding but distant possibility—when the future identity of this continent was still up for grabs. In 1845 nobody knew whether the North or South would prove victorious; accordingly, Reichardt's film lacks all moral certainty. There is no quest to impose capitalism. There is hardly even a plot. All we have are seven people trying to find their way out of a self-imposed wilderness. Their flight, doubt, emptiness, ambiguity.

DIMINISHED EXPECTATIONS

Rousseau wanted a logical argument. He wanted to discover some method of persuading a people why their government should rule.

He hammered out this question in 1762 and never answered it to his satisfaction; to my knowledge no one ever has. Some 250 years later, the political philosopher Simon Critchley decided to admit defeat. Instead of answering Rousseau's riddle, he wove the impossibility of ever solving this question into the body of his own philosophy. The catch in Rousseau's catch-22 is the point. He calls it the "paradox of sovereignty": you *have to* invent some sort of legitimate authority in order to make laws that people will follow. This is how human governance works.

This certainly puts things into perspective. No longer do the intellectuals of Western civilization aspire to square the circle of governance. We no longer build utopian dreams. To the contrary, we live in divided times amid problems that can't be solved. Our world is ruled by arguments that rage on like infernos, and we will never put them out.

TEDIUM

With all these lengthy, static shots of the settlers moving slowly West, it is quickly becoming evident that the settling of the frontier is dull. The common denominator in *Meek's Cutoff* is this sense of slow transition. This tedious walk West is the physical embodiment of what we find everywhere in this film: the in-between spaces, the unmapped gaps.

Rebecca Solnit: "To be lost is to be fully present, and to be fully present is to be capable of being in uncertainty and mystery."

The whole scenario of this film is one gigantic in-between, dots struggling through unlimited white space. This is what lets Reichardt tear the Western apart. Without plot points, no one knows if we're moving forward or backward, who is good and who is evil. By running her camera for such long takes, Reichardt moves beyond the figurehead ideas to see the anxiety beneath them.

A PLOT?

The logic of going West is possessing these people. They're no longer traveling for any particular reason. Now they go West because they've been going West so long that going West is all they know. It has become what they are.

And they are running out of water. Drop by drop, their reserves are growing small. Nobody knows when next it will be found.

All the while Reichardt adds slabs of marble to the monument she is building to the magnificence of these grand regions. Her perspective is elemental, the land is overpowering.

The settlers trek through a place severed from the world. They are so perfectly free.

Typically the Western imagines such rampant freedom as a war of the fittest, Good and Bad shooting it out at noon. But this condescends to the true freedom that people settling an unconquered land must have felt, that dizzying emptiness that comes with disconcerting spaces. This is what Reichardt achieves with these long, still shots of her tiny people treading an immense path.

This is a depiction of freedom that must be seen. One of the most severe flaws of the American project is that we believe we understand what freedom is. Watching *Meek's Cutoff*, it is clear we have only begun.

TWO GUNSHOTS

Susan Sontag: "[The] genius of American capitalism is that anything that becomes known in this country becomes assimilated."

The sequence where the settlers first meet the Native is extraordinary. Reichardt does something that many filmmakers would never dare, for fear of offending their audience—she takes her time. There are no frantic jump-cuts, no chaotic shifting of perspectives, no hand-held, point-of-view running sequences. Reichardt does it all in long, laborious mid-length shots.

Emily Tetherow is out collecting firewood, and Reichardt's camera is drawing in on her walking feet. The shot tightens, and we see Emily's hands come into the frame as she bends down to collect the wood. The camera explores just a tiny bit of the dead space ahead of her, to indicate something is about to appear. It is a classic opening.

First contact: Emily's skirts are beside the Native's leathered legs. The camera starts panning up as though to reveal his face, but before it can get there Reichardt cuts to a three-quarters shot of Emily standing in dumb terror, arms full of dry wood. For one elongated moment we see her staring into the Native's eyes, but, crucially, Reichardt never shows us how his face regards hers. We are forced to empathize with Emily, we cannot even guess how the Native stares back.

The next sequence proves Reichardt's status. Emily dashes back to the camp and leaps into the covered wagon. The other women in the distance are yelling inaudible remarks. Ignoring them fully, she hops back out with a gun and begins the laborious process of firing it. We hear her heaving breath, her grunts of exertion. We watch her concentration, the calm that comes with crisis. The three figures in the distance jostle with anxiety. For ten full seconds Emily ministers to the weapon—when it finally does fire, the crack is like a slap. The shot goes high, high up into the sky, alerting the men to come back to camp *immediately*. And then something even more profound: for nearly a full minute Emily reloads the gun. She empties, cleans, loads, cocks. Reichardt just leaves us there, helplessly watching. The cord of emergency pulls tighter and tighter until—with a second crack the frame goes full black, we hear Meek's quiet voice questioning Emily. Flickering firelight indicates that it is hours later.

With this sequence, Reichardt forces me to see how terror can be a prosaic emotion, drawing more from boredom than novelty. How it can accompany the everyday stuff of living. This is a kind of terror like the empty, desiccated terrain of the Western wilderness. Reichardt's settlers traverse this mundane, omnipresent terror, as do we stalk through a terror so quotidian that it lacks signpost or map, an undefined state of anxiety that for all we know may end tomorrow or extend to the end of our days.

CLARITY CAME SLOWLY

Years passed and I learned to see my nation anew.

I marched in the protests against the Iraq War. I learned

of the crimes in Guantanamo and Abu Ghraib. I listened to the meager rhetoric used to expropriate the nation's wealth. I watched the debacle in New Orleans. I heard the men and women of government line up to denounce the welfare state that had established their country as the most modern and powerful on Earth. I saw the nation shrug and accept complete electronic surveillance.

Congress changed hands, the next President came. Some things became better, but many problems remained intractable. New wars. New cuts. New debacles. New ways to spy and kill.

In those years I began to understand that the project of the United States did not complete in the 19th century, nor in the 20th. The country still was very young; even compared to the rather youthful nations of Western Europe it was just an adolescent. Hardly battle-tried, its future not assured. To the contrary, the only thing we could count on were bitter trials. These upcoming crises would likely be tests of equal or greater gravity than those we had already survived.

I continued to read the political philosophers that I had become acquainted with at university. I added new thinkers to my bookshelves. I saw more and more of this enormous nation. I saw more of the world. I watched many, many films.

Through all of those years, work, war, and terror were never far from my sight.

OUTCASTS SCARE RULERS

What does a society do with the people who will not fit into the way of life it wants to establish as normal? What do those outcasts do with the society that will not accept them?

How do problems first arise between the society and its outcasts?

How do they develop?

What finally resolves them?

After Emily shoots her weapon and informs the men of her encounter, there is a makeshift manhunt, and at length the Native is captured. This is mere prologue to the dilemma of what to do with him. Meek wants murder. Others hope he can lead them to the dearly needed water. Some try to teach him about trading and property. Some want to set him free.

Unable to agree, they eventually do the very worst thing: they ignore him. Thus do problems become toxic.

Rod Rondeaux's Native stands inscrutable as an ancient stele; through all the settlers' ministrations his face remains ambiguous. This mystery becomes a source of power. It fascinates the settlers. The Native's enigma encourages them to question Meek's claims. Simply by presenting an alternative, the Native is undermining the regime on which Meek's authority rests.

AGORAPHOBIA

Not long after they capture the Native, Meek says with horror, "we've come to a terrible place."

Whiteout. The fright of being lost in open space. Of being permitted to move, but to know that this motion is pointless. Traveling forward is the one thing that assures us of our vitality. When we move forward, we know that we are going somewhere. We have a purpose. But when every horizon looks the same, our lives become futile.

To quell the building panic, Meek tries to give some assurance of direction. It is as though Reichardt's film is asking us to examine just how badly we need narrative.

Rebecca Solnit: "Love, wisdom, grace, inspiration—how do you go about finding these things that are in some ways about extending the boundaries of the self into unknown territory, about becoming someone else?"

Reichardt knows that nowadays we cannot become lost in a spatial sense. We all have maps and global positioning systems on our phones. But there are other wildernesses to wander into. Reichardt indicates the one she thinks we are lost in. She sneaks into her movie numerous references toward our own sense of rudderless national morass. She asks us to reconsider our legitimizing myths. To confront the uncertainty of not knowing where we are headed.

CRISIS

Now Reichardt brings us toward crisis. Meek and his charges continue arguing about the fate of the Native, the water grows smaller, the fact of being lost becomes undeniable. One wrong move will ignite this situation.

The party comes upon a steep ravine. The Native scrambles up to it and begins talking frantically. No one knows a word of what he says, but they become convinced that he is telling them that on the other side, just beyond that hill, there is water. If they can just navigate the ravine, they might be saved. But the ravine is much too steep for the wagons, it's suicide to try and pass.

Is it a trick? Is the Native trying to trick them into chancing the steep ravine? Or is there really water just within reach? The settlers sap their remaining strength in arguments, and perhaps it is because of their exhaustion that they make the desperate choice to let their wagons down inch by inch from a rope, bracing all they possess against their accumulated weight, their depleted energy.

DECISIONS

What does the Native think as he sits and watches the settlers lower all they possess into a sheer pit? Does he have any idea how much these people value this property? Can a nomad conceive of the sense of identity wrapped around these things?

Two wagons descend without incident, but with the third

comes catastrophe. The settlers lose their grip. For one helpless moment they watch it skitter down and topple over. A total loss.

And right here, right here is where Rod Rondeaux earns his paycheck. As the destruction unfurls, Reichardt cuts to a close-up of his head. His face wears a perfectly inscrutable, perfectly ambiguous expression. Is this uncomprehending curiosity? Bemusement? Pleasure? Malice? Boredom? Does he realize the devastation?

And what about Meek and his settlers: how much of the rest of their lives are determined right at this juncture?

RONDEAUX'S EYES

You can hold Rondeaux's expression frozen before your eyes, as I have done, for minutes at a time; you can replay the scene time and again, as I have also done. But you cannot answer the question: what is his intent?

In this failure to read the face of this inscrutable man, the film inverts: I understand how the Native has felt this whole time, attempting to comprehend these settlers. Trying to read their faces, understand their motives. Knowing not what they mean to do with him. There is only ambiguity.

Meek, of course, doesn't care to read the Native's face. He is quite convinced that the Native has set him up, and he will do something about it. The destruction of property will be his justification for murder. But as he raises his gun in execution, Emily raises the same shotgun she used crack off her two terrible warning shots, and she aims it at Meek. Drop your weapon, she says with a steady voice.

"Well maybe you'd like to wager water for blood," Meek hisses as he lowers his weapon.

It's possible to read this as Reichardt finally bending under the pressures of genre and imposing moral certainty on her story. It is also the closest she comes to openly declaring the many parallels between the events of her film and what began happening in the United States on September 11, 2001.

Here is what I see in Emily's decision: I see her making the cut that finally severs the umbilical. A cut that has been too long in coming. Emily has done the unthinkable. She has declared what nobody wanted to declare. They must all now live with her choice.

THE CONSEQUENCE

Much about my life remained the same after that September morning. I maintained my habits, I did not change my aspirations. I was still basically the same person. I imagined this level-headedness as individuality. I would not let the mounting fear and paranoia inflect my life. I would continue to be me.

But the world around me was shifting. This, I think, is what alarmed me most about that day. On some level I had to have known that I could not escape this new world. With my permission or not, it would take me with it.

Despite my rigorous attempts to maintain my integrity, I lived in a world that had established a new normality. These new regulations, these new processes and politicians, these transformed political parties and debates—who can now remember exactly why they were implemented, what aims they were meant to satisfy, who they served? They are just part of life now. So do civilizations age.

Robert Pogue Harrison: "Genuine newness entails the rejuvenation, rather than the repudiation, of that from which it seeks freedom and independence."

I have tried to show grace in accepting what cannot be changed and integrity in preserving what should not be changed. But the question that day unleashed, the question that the sight of the falling towers put into me—this question still remains. Whether or not I want it to, the world continues to bring back my memories of where I was that day, and how I felt. I remember the morning on which this question first echoed in my ears.

The wagon's fall, that September morning, this question. They are all right there, all exactly together.

A CONCLUSION OF SORTS

The film ends as ambiguous as ever. The settlers recover, they set out again, they find a tree. Trees imply water, but this one is a rather pathetic, saggy kind of tree, and it may well be dead. Perhaps the water that once fed it is long gone. The settlers may die, or they may yet survive.

Beckett: "Unfathomable mind, now beacon, now sea."

If this is indeed the Tree of Life that they've reached, Eden's had a rough time. But as an emblem of that thing each of them is seeking in running away, the tree feels right: it is an authentic discovery, but it is fragile, ambiguous. Interpreting it will take some time.

In the final shot we see the Native stalking off into the distance. Perhaps the discord he brought became too much trouble and they have let him go. Perhaps they've realized the absurdity of holding a captive while you yourself are hopelessly lost in the captive's world. Perhaps they've simply lost interest in him. Perhaps, perhaps, perhaps. We never learn if the Native had a tribe, if he will go back to those he knows or will simply stay in the wilderness, alone forever. Here, as the film melts away to black, as the Native walks off, we are shown another kind of life: a different freedom, a permanent state of exile, a radical foreignness. A different path. Certainly not the one we have chosen. Reichardt has let us dwell in it for some 97 minutes.

2011, HORRIFIED AND SYMPATHETIC
The Seventh Continent, Michael Haneke (1989)

A hand scoops coffee. An eye blinks. Gas is pumped. Teeth are brushed. Never full-bodied human beings, never willful agents pursuing their own lives. Bits and pieces operating, being operated upon. Inert documentary chunks suited to the mechanical life they portray.

The first scenes seem so innocent.

The family sits in their car as it is pushed through the carwash. They are placid, plastered, swaddled within four thousand pounds of steel. The carwash is a dark trench. The car is carried through on tracks. The sense of mechanization is overwhelming.

All this built simply so that decent people shouldn't have to scrape the grime off their own car.

It is just another thing people do. Millions of them, every day.

It is all part of a normal life.

Being dragged through a dark trench with your family in stuporous silence, a gaze devoid of any sense on all your faces.

What do they think, the father, the mother, the little girl, each trapped in their own fine skull? The only people we see amid all this swimming machinery.

As the car rolls out of the carwash, there is a sign advertising vacations to Australia. A beautiful, sandy beach. Bright sun.

Hélène Cixous: "One sends messages to oneself hidden in the form of symptoms."

Soon after, the little girl feigns blindness at school. The teacher informs the mother, who, with great anger, tries to force the little girl to confess. She will not. She tries a different approach. My little dear, do not be afraid, just tell mommy the truth and it will be okay. So then she tells. The mother slaps her crisply. What anger, what hatred of one's own life in that slap.

The husband and wife shop for groceries in the local supermarket, but it is the shopping cart, not them, that holds the center of the frame. We never see the shopper's heads, only their arms and legs as they manipulate their nutrition into their cart. Shopping is dehumanizing, it is robotic; when I later see them eat their steak and drink their wine, I know it gives them no pleasure.

At the table the wife's brother, who is staying with them for a few weeks, breaks down into tears for no reason. The little girl is confused and afraid. The adults seem no better equipped to comprehend what is happening. No one extends a hand.

They have a huge aquarium as big as a wall stocked with exotic fish. Every so often we see a family member drop in fish food, and the quick response as the fish dart upward on a diagonal.

The fish swim because they cannot do otherwise. They eat the food because it is given.

The husband edges out his superior at work. He is making good money in a stable job, they have a sizable inheritance from the wife's parents. They will keep the inheritance in the bank so as not to be taxed on it.

Money is no problem.

Every day they wake at 6:00 am to the same news broadcast, the same toothbrushings, the same coffee and cereal. Even the key in their bedroom door has not moved an inch in a year. They sit in their same car in the same carwash.

Day in and day out. The same. The same. The same. Life lived simply because it *must* be lived, because there is no other choice.

Barthes: "Why is the viable a Good Thing? Why is it better to *last* than to *burn*?"

There are the saved and the doomed, and Haneke's people are the latter. They are incapable of obsessing over the must-be-livedness of life. Incapable of dissecting the absurdity of being thrown here. What permits us to go on.

What pain in what can never be expressed.

Yet they do go on. It is all they do. This is the horror of their lives. They have not yet grasped this horror, but it is there.

I sense it all flowing along some channel, but when does it change? When does it start to break and rage? When does their deranged intentionality dawn upon me? *Oh yes, now, things are being done for a reason.*

And as I sit here on my couch, finally guessing just what this film is about, all of the horror of fascination emboldening my senses, I can already tell that the woman I love, sitting right here next to me, her attention with this movie is flailing, sleep is coming upon her, her head is growing heavier on my shoulder. I think this is for the best.

Something awful must be contained within their purpose. Something abysmal that must exist. Because if it does not exist, life is canned. Now that these people are finally bending toward this awful thing, their lives at last have some meaning.

This thing is why Haneke made his movie. To show us this essential facet of our world. This thing inside this horrific scheme inside them.

Let me break it down:

Here's what Slavoj Žižek says Lacan believes: basically three things rule the human world. These things are:

1) people like ourselves

2) the "big Other,"—society, codes of conduct, laws, etc., the contrivances we've made to govern ourselves

3) the "Thing," i.e. God, Truth, Being, whatever you'll call that little word Beckett can never quite name

Žižek says that while we're off having our relations with (1), relations that only work because of, and are determined by (2), what really makes it all possible is the creeping suspicion that somewhere out there we'll get to meet (3). But if we can't bring ourselves to believe in (3), then we're done. "We find ourselves in a 'flat' aseptic universe in which subjects are . . . reduced to lifeless pawns in the regulated game of communication."

And there you have it. Lifeless pawns in the regulated game of communication. Dehumanized. Machines.

But what if (3) isn't beauty, isn't love, isn't nobility? What if your (3) is disgusting?

A year later: the wife is in the carwash again, smothered in a shadow black as night. We see her profile, but not a single feature of her face. The shot shifts to the husband, indicating we have just seen his point of view. The shot jumps back to the wife, who is moaning uncontrollably in a fit of sobs. The husband sits and watches. The car shifts by the advertisement for Australia.

They take their daughter to see the husband's parents. His elderly father and mother smile. They have reached life's end, have outlasted the horrors of the 20th century. They bid their son goodbye and ask that he drive home carefully. We see him dangerously passing cars on the snowy road. Someone puts out a bowl of cereal for the little girl and sprinkles a generous amount of sugar on top. She eats half of it and declares herself full. Mother tucks her in, the little girl asks God to watch her soul should she not wake.

The husband writes a letter to his parents: he did not want to say it during the visit, but he has decided to quit his job. The scene shifts and they are at the bank, withdrawing the inheritance. Are they in need of money? the teller asks. They might take a loan instead, it might make more sense financially. They tell him they are emigrating.

To Australia.

And now the head that rests against my shoulder is quite heavy, she has definitely fallen asleep. I do not want her to wake up, not at all. I want to watch happen what will happen, I need to see this film reach its grotesque end, I want to be in this spell alone. I do not want her to witness this horror, and nor do I want her to intrude upon it either. If she awakes it breaks.

They write to the husband's parents. They have had a tough time deciding, but they will take their daughter with them. In church the little girl said she was not afraid of death. It is a sign she should come with them.

As we hear these words we see the daughter coloring in an abstract drawing.

Is Haneke telling me that humans make art, which means we are not animals, and that therefore we deserve dignity and meaning? Or is he saying that this how humans pass their life, carefully filling in the forms given them?

Hebrews 11:1: "Now faith is the substance of things hoped for, and the evidence of things unseen."

It all happens fast now. For the second time we see the mother at the doctor filling her prescription.

The father buys severe tools: a sledgehammer, a power saw, an axe.

The mother buys an exorbitant array of delicacies. The shopgirl asks her who is getting married. No one. It is just for them to enjoy. Oh, she replies, then they are having people over? The mother is consuming a rich chocolate when the girl asks, and as she swallows it, she snaps at her: No. There is no occasion.

The husband sells his car. At the junkyard we hear dissonant music playing from the car stereo. It is Alban Berg, "To the Memory of An Angel," virtually the only "soundtrack" in this movie.

Alban Berg was capable of finding meaning in the death of an innocent young woman.

It is though Haneke is challenging us.

They take a cab home and in an extended point of view shot we see the husband take a long stare down one end of his street and then down the other.

How many times he has stared down this street? How many times you have stared down your street? But this time with the knowledge that it will never be done again.

What passes through his head in these instants?

Perhaps the sense that at last life is worth living. At last he has found a purpose to excite his being. These last few weeks he has felt an engagement with the world that has always been missing.

Lacan: "Knowledge is worth just as much as it costs."

As they eat their dinner the phone rings. The husband takes it off its cradle and lets it hang by the cord.

The next morning the mother is setting out an enormous platter of rich cheeses. There is a crash from the living room. The husband has crushed the shelf above the TV with the sledgehammer. If we are to have a chance, he says, we must be systematic.

Systematic destruction. Yes, Michael Haneke surely knows who else engaged in systematic destruction.

They eat a gluttonous breakfast. They sip wine even as they fill their coffee cups. There are rolls, butter, chocolates, cheese, fruit.

What meaning does this food have for them? How does it taste?

With chilling deliberation the husband picks up the top shirt off a stack of shirts and cleanly rips it down the middle, spilling the buttons on the floor. Then the next, and the next, and the next. It is utterly controlled, but the violence is unmistakable.

The anger.

How he loathes those shirts.

Cold, dispassionate rage.

And I still feel her heavy head upon my shoulder, hear her regular, deep breaths, and I think that all that separates me from these people is the ceasing of this breath.

They rip every last piece of clothing to tatters with the same methodical violence. They snap records in half. They tear up photo albums. They pull down the curtains and eviscerate them. They destroy the little girl's drawings. We see the abstract drawing she had worked on earlier as it is torn firmly in half. We, of course, recognize it, just as we recognize that they do not.

It is a bitter and fascistically thorough renunciation of the very fact that they have ever walked the earth.

We must have a system if we are to achieve our aim.

They move from small to big. They bash the TV into itself. They hammer chests of drawers to splinters. They buzzsaw their walls.

There is silence but for the sound of their work.

Not a sound at all but the whisper of demolition.

This work goes on and on.

The mother screams NO! While the voice still resounds, the scene cuts from her twisted mouth to a shot of the husband swinging his axe through the glass wall of the fish tank.

It is a brilliant moment. At one stroke the entirety of what is happening is punctuated, sublimated, and embodied.

The entire film is here.

Water floods the room. Shots of the dying fish trying desperately to flip themselves back into their life. Desperate agony. The little girl runs into the room. She is immediately in hysterics. The mother holds her back as she attempts to scramble over the broken glass and clutch the dying fish. The scene goes on and on, the little girl screaming, screaming.

I want to tell her: please, do not prolong this atrocity.

I just want this to be over with.

Why do I not just stop the film right here? It is obvious what remains to be done. Why do I force myself to see this?

Do I want to see it happen? Am I intrigued?

Somewhere in me, do I agree?

The fish's thrashings become slower and slower. They strain for life with complete futility, and this makes them poignant.

No living thing really wants to die.

Do this man and woman feel doubt? This is their one chance.

Shots of the house in tatters.

Someone is at the door. The husband stalks up to it like a thief.

A representative of the phone company. It is not permitted to leave one's phone off the hook. It interferes with the line. The husband apologizes quite sincerely and says he will replace it immediately.

Might they come in to have a look at it? they ask.

No, he says.

They flush money down the toilet. Hundreds of thousands of marks. Enough to live a good life. It goes on and on.

It is as though they are flushing away the years of hard work.

Haneke: "There were people who left the cinema, slamming the doors. Everywhere I showed the film, that was the main scene people complained about. It's a lot less disturbing if parents kill their children and themselves than if they destroy their money."

They watch a cover of Celine Dion's ballad "The Power of Love" in their darkened living room to pass the time as they wait for their little girl to succumb to the poison they have told her to drink.

It's bitter, she says, so trustingly.

Why Celine Dion? Because it is so unbearably and universally beloved. Mass culture has no answers. It cannot even offer us comfort. All it can do is help pass the time spent waiting for death.

The wife is next. She dissolves the pills with the butt end of her toothbrush. She moves with such impatience, as if annoyed that her poison takes so long to prepare. She slugs it with such rancor that it spills out the sides of her mouth. We see her shuddering in her death throes over the body of her little girl,

186

and it seems as though at the very last moment she has realized it was all a terrible mistake.

The husband cannot keep his poison down. He keeps vomiting it up.

To be the last alive. What thoughts would one have?

What if one wanted to live?

What knowledge contained in this moment?

He goes to the bathroom and fills a syringe to inject himself.

He sits in a stupor staring at a TV, its static a stand-in for his fuzzing consciousness. As the camera zooms into the static, cuts to previous shots from the movie. His wife sobbing uncontrollably. His daughter smiling.

Last thoughts before death? The very last thought he has?

How impossible, how despicable to think that anyone would ever have a last thought.

That I will have a last thought.

That this heavy head, this most cherished mind will have a last thought.

That mine might be of her.

That it might be of she and I on a Greek island staring at a sunset that I told myself in that moment I'd like to be the last thing I ever think about.

A coda tells us that despite a suicide note and no evidence to the contrary, the father's father insisted it was murder. He simply would not believe his son and daughter-in-law could do this.

This is the real father's father who said this.

The father of the Austrians who actually did this.

What are we to make of Haneke's story? There is no hint that redemption is a possibility. There is no indication of why they did it. There is only documentation of the world that drove them to death and their immense hatred of it.

How long did they harbor these feelings? What finally

put them on the path to suicide? Why them and not someone else?

Or, I suppose, what I really mean to ask: Why are they different from me?

2014, ONE REQUIRES A WALL

Exit Through the Gift Shop, Banksy (2010)

I will always be envious of artists because they can create with their entire body.

Words do not work like this. It doesn't matter whether I'm standing on my head as I type this sentence or sitting here on my ass. It all looks the same to you as you read it.

But look at the kinetics on the first two-and-a-half minutes of this movie. People painting with gouging torches, streaming down subway tunnels, perched high atop skyscrapers, standing out the windows of moving cars, shooting paint out of hoses. I crave this—art plus gymnastics, art plus muay thai, art plus zero to sixty. Art made on the level of muscle memory.

The last image in this opening montage, almost something out of *The Matrix*. In a white T-shirt he skids away from the cops, and he runs right up the side of a building. The plump law can't make so much as an honest effort at pulling itself up in pursuit.

This art is what Michael Jordan's 1988, free-throw-line slam dunk would look like if it could have made an imprint on a wall.

Some days when I've ran beneath the blazing spring sun, legs aflame, the hill at last climbed and below me the entire city, the blue waters of the ocean, I feel this ecstasy. I wish there were a way I could write with that vigor.

Can there be any doubt that street art is a full body experience? It is done in the wee hours when the city's empty streets are a playground. Even as the hand sprays, the five senses are always on high alert. Perched atop a ledge it would be nothing to fall down and die, or find a subway car screaming through the tunnel, or be chest down in gravel beneath a tractor trailer as a police helicopter pulses overhead.

After that brassy overture, who appears on the screen? Or rather: who does *not* appear? Body and face obscured beneath baggy jeans and an enormous hoodie casting deep shadows, voice encoded, sitting next to an ironic monkey's face.

He says: "The film is the story of what happened when this guy tried to make a documentary about me. But he was actually a lot more interesting that I am."

All of Banksy's bodily expressions are concentrated into his two hands. They are the only parts of him given any definition whatsoever. This street artist *par excellence* embodies the gestural minimalism of an oracle.

Mystery is Banksy's first asset. He has invested his career in its perfection. He is a hugely famous artist, even though very few people know his name, a man who spent years dodging the police as he built his reputation in graffiti, only to see the entire movement catch on to glowing incandescence, his whole art and life legitimized by the beneficent nod of the market that has made him a millionaire.

The screen flips to this other man, this Thierry Guetta, everything that Banksy is not: a buffoon, a babbler, a self-aggrandizer always in pursuit of the spotlight. He does not obscure his face beneath a gigantic hood. He wears a moustache that connects to two ludicrous muttonchops. He fidgets endlessly. Everything about this man begs you to look at him and remember him.

What Thierry does is film. The way you or I peer with our eyeballs, Thierry films with his camera.

Who is this movie really about? Is it about Banksy, or Thierry? And what is the truth of either of these men? Just a few minutes in, and already there is something undeniably artificial about each. This Banksy, his hoodie so compellingly distressed, the warehouse-like studio behind him perfectly arranged in its disorder. And this Thierry, so aptly, absolutely naïve in his jackassery.

As Banksy puts it, "I guess Thierry was in the right place at the right time, really. We all needed someone who knew how to use a camera."

Very soon, these opposites are to meet and become collaborators.

Michael Taussig: "Defacement works on objects the way jokes work on language, bringing out their inherent magic nowhere more so than when those objects have become routinized and social."

Whatever else it is, *Exit Through the Gift Shop* is an outstanding advertisement for Banksy and the genre of art he makes. Which would put it in line with virtually all the art of Banksy's I've ever seen, all those morbidly sarcastic, lightly subversive, clip art–esque stencils spraypainted up on city walls. For someone in love with anonymity—for someone famous for *never* showing his face ever for any reason—he certainly has a passion for branding. This film is no different. He drove around America graffitiing the countryside as part of the publicity campaign. When it was nominated for an Oscar for Best Documentary the rumors began to swirl: would Banksy finally show his face? As the saying goes, you can't buy that kind of publicity.

It's all a little too perfect in that Banksy sort of way: something in me dearly wants to believe in him, but everything about this man is very, very hard to swallow.

Speaking of too perfect, as the film starts it's the early 2000s, and Thierry discovers that his cousin is a full-on street artist named Invader. He could not have happened along at a better time! As Rhys Ifan's voice-over puts it amid a fancy montage of Invader's work, "street art was poised to become the biggest countercultural movement since punk, and Thierry had landed right in the middle of it." Cousin Invader invites Thierry on some bombing runs, and this is Thierry's initiation into the world of street art, that first tiny step in his inevitable collision with Banksy.

True to his name, Invader uses little square tiles to reconstruct pixelated characters from 8-bit video games like *Space Invaders*, and then he glues them up in unobtrusive places all over major cities. Invader started doing this in the mid-90s, which means his mosaics are retro art. In that decade, 8-bit graphics just weren't being made any longer. They were already a long-dead style, like art deco or beehives.

I'm a member of the last generation that grew up when these images were in style. I have foggy memories of playing an Atari in the early '80s, and I have very good memories of the Nintendo Entertainment System that replaced it. Eight-bit graphics are part of my cultural memory. But the generations that came after me got better video game systems with better graphics, and when they see Invader's 8-bit mosaics, they only really them as a vintage style. They have a vague sense of what his art is supposed to represent, but they don't really recognize the source.

Street art relies on the compressed cycles of late capitalism, because it needs a never-ending supply of iconic vintage like the 8-bit *Space Invader* graphics. It absolutely feasts on the fifteen-minute icons created by modern advertising campaigns and Internet memes, things like the Old Spice Man or lolcats. Street art's quintessential experience is that déjà vu moment when you happen to notice something that shouldn't be there. That flash of insight that makes you feel like you're in on something. The punch that comes from the interplay between the art and its surroundings, that shocking second when the dull cityscape momentarily feels cool.

This is what makes for a memorable street art style. If the style is good, then the more you see it, the more you begin to notice it everywhere. The more you *want* to notice it everywhere. And the more you want to know what it's all about.

This is viral is it not? The YouTube video that becomes famous because it has racked up a billion views.

In Banksy's words: "All you need now is a few ideas and a broadband connection."

Minimalist statements building up an edifice of authenticity and mystique. It's what ad campaigns get mocked for failing to pull off.

A kind of art that's native to our historical moment, where we all sort of feel like everything kind of sucks. It's this endemic dissatisfaction with the perceived falseness of day-to-day life that alienates us from technocrats controlling our democracies.

To put it all another way: when I see Invader's mosaics, I know they don't belong there. I like them for precisely that reason, and they make me wonder why it takes a felonious gesture to make the city a little less depressing, why the people who run the city can't make it suck a little less on their own. And this question treads toward some emerging thought on the tip of everybody's tongue. This is what good art has tended to do in the modern era: it lets the mass culture know what it's thinking before it's quite able to say it.

If I feel close to the street art movement, it's because we came along at virtually the same time. Its star commodities are just a few years older than I am. Always just a smidgen ahead of me, they were creating the fads that I came of age in. I appreciate their insight into why this world is dissatisfying. I get their jokes, I understand their love of authenticity, their hatred of phonies, I feel their tension between making it and staying real. Their methods are the methods I have tried to use in my own way as a writer, their values are by and large my values. I love the ecstasy I see when I watch them create.

And Banksy—their five-star general!—my archetype of the self-made artist. An artist so successful that for him making art is akin to printing money. This is the ultimate: the artist who can do whatever he wants. The artist who has escaped the need for a career.

The artist with fuck-you money. This is what I dream of.

There are people out there who despise Banksy. Some of my closest friends have aired their grievances during tipsy nights in trendy bars. The artist himself claims that he once sat in a theater during a preview of this film, and someone yelled at the screen, "OH MY GOD, BANKSY IS SUCH A SELL-OUT." Perhaps. Even if you can never quite pick out the bullshit from the sincerity with Banksy, this story bespeaks a certain uneasiness with his enormous success.

But it is equally true that Banksy has inspired the sort of fervid excitement that few artists in the modern era can muster. One in a myriad of such inspiration: those fake Paris Hilton albums he deposited in record stores in place of the real Paris Hilton album. He even pre-installed them with subtly re-touched, slightly pornographic images of Hilton, with song titles like "What Am I For?," plus deep thoughts straight from the heiress, like "Every CD you buy puts me even further out of your league." What hater could possibly suppress a little grudging smirk?

But of course, these CDs could just be another brick in the edifice of self. The self-made, shit-eating grin'd slacker antihero who knows what you don't. All of his little slights to the ruling order might just be in service to building the Banksy aura. An enigma who hunkers down under an enormous hoodie and creates vicious ways of speaking truth to power from construction paper, razor blades, and compressed paint.

That's the Banksy image.

I'd like to believe it's real, but it's a little hard to swallow.

Gabriella Coleman: "[Among the ranks of Anonymous,] drawing attention and fame to one's name is the ultimate taboo."

I feel so much less ambiguous about this guy named Shepard Fairey, this man who just emanates charismatic chill despite his barber-school haircut, his ill-fitting cargo pants, threadbare T-shirt, and big Midwestern grin. Fairey always makes me think of an adolescent's sense of sinful fun trapped in the mind of a full-grown man.

He's such a cool guy that he up and adopts Thierry sight unseen, simply because Invader says he's all right. Assuming this story isn't complete bullshit, this is an exemplary lesson in how authority works in the creative world.

And what do Thierry and Fairey do together? Well, Fairey gambols around LA putting up his OBEY posters, and Thierry videotapes him with his ever-present camera. He even helps Fairey do his thing from time to time. Thierry and Fairey go *everywhere* together, and it looks like great fun. Fairey begins sharing this ever-present camera with his friends, and they love him too. They've all been putting up this great stuff in decaying cityscapes around the world, and for years they've watched the inevitable processes of erosion, bureaucracy, and rivalry take it back down. And now here's Thierry, a guy who has no scruples whatsoever about following Shaquille O'Neill around LA and just sticking his camera in the man's face until Shaq finally has to growl at him. In other words a guy with almost no self-awareness, no filters, nothing. A guy with as much nerve as you could possibly have. What could possibly go wrong?

From the omega to the alpha: we bounce back to Banksy, finding him in the Tate Britain of all places, home to some of the most expensive, most classic art in all of Europe. What's he doing there? He's sticking up his own art. Banksy doesn't come to the Tate to stare at the Turners and the Bacons and the Blakes, he comes to look for a little empty space in between them where he can stick up his own nonsense. He's brought along a little painting of the bucolic British countryside that he bought at a flea market and doctored up with some yellow police tape. He's even got a placard to go with it. So he sticks them right in Room Seven of the Tate Britain. And of course it plays on the six o'clock news and everyone loves it.

Shitting right on the emperor's throne and getting away scot free. That's Banksy.

Or perhaps I should say: giving the impression of having shat right on the throne and gotten away scot free, story on the six o'clock news.

But he's not done yet. Not only does he hit the Tate, which at the worst would get you a severe talking to by one of those bored guards. No, he goes somewhere where there's a much higher degree of danger. He graffitis the wall the Israelis have built on the West Bank. And, of course, he's taken care to bring his cameraman with him here, too, because there's plenty of video footage for distribution to all the major outlets.

A funny thing: watching this film, you can't help but get the impression that Banksy is the first person on Earth to have hit the West Bank. But then you snoop around the Internet and you see that many, many people have done the exact same thing—people who haven't gotten a millionth the exposure as Banksy did out of it. So many, in fact, that there's a 329-page monograph on the art of the West Bank wall selling on Amazon for $169.95.

Regardless. The West Bank is not enough for Banksy. For now we see him in LA, his first show ever in the United States. And who is the guest of honor? It's an elephant! Yes, at his own show Banksy has given up the spotlight to an "elephant in the room." Right on cue, in swoop the humorless animal rights' people, who instantly condemn him for covering the creature in make-up, and then some bobblehead news reporters show up to cover the controversy, and before you know it Banksy has the kind of publicity you can't buy.

This is Banksy's genius: he inserts himself into the master narratives of the day and leverages the fuck out of them. He knows how to turn his creations into a media spectacle, while he himself wanders off as though oblivious.

Banksy draws you in with the dare of it: the nerve to touch the live wires we've all been taught to avoid at any cost. I remember when I was a child in school, and there was always that one classmate who just wouldn't stop prodding the teacher.

I couldn't believe he was getting away with it. I was dying to see how far he could go! Banksy knows that the power relationship is 100 percent asymmetrical: he knows he's never going to bring down the wall on the West Bank; he's never going to upset the hegemony of the Tate over the art world. He's just the guy who's willing to point all this out, to shock us out of our complacency for a minute and say, *well, isn't this world we live in just a little too sick to believe?* To quote the man himself: "We can't do anything to change the world until capitalism crumbles. In the meantime, we should all go shopping to console ourselves."

This is fine entertainment, it's even not too bad as agit-prop, but is it art? Other than titillating the malcontented slackers of the world, exactly what good does Banksy's work do? Sure, it's fun to look at, but it also has a tendency to assault you with its irony. It's not exactly an invitation into inquiry or sustained reflection. One might even go so far as to say that in casting some levity over a generally depressing state of affairs, in giving the would-be mobs of late capitalism a valve for blowing off a little steam, Banksy's work may do more to make the ruling order palatable than to vandalize it.

But anyway: Banksy's plan works. The Tate, the wall in Palestine, the LA show, together they ignite a raging wildfire of market interest in street art. As the voice-over says, pretty soon "no serious contemporary art collection would be complete without a Banksy."

Or a Shepard Fairey. Or an Invader. And on and on and on. They're all selling in the tens of thousands of dollars.

And there's Thierry, filming it with his camera and making a plan.

You have to hand it to Banksy. The guy may become filthy rich, but he doesn't lose his edge. After the market for his work reaches ludicrous levels of white hot, he makes a piece simply titled "Morons." It's a print of wealthy collectors bidding on a framed canvas that says "I CAN'T BELIEVE YOU MORONS ACTUALLY BUY THIS SHIT."

The piece sold rather well.

And this is that ultimate, unsurpassable level of success: no matter what Banksy does, there's a line of people around the block to buy it. Even when he produces a print custom-designed to insult the intelligence of the people who buy his work, they still love it. This is the immaculate thing about prodigies like Banksy. They create fortunes with their own two hands. They do not mass produce, they do not conduct extensive market research, they do not run ad campaigns or create distribution schemes. They just paint.

Who in this over-worked, penny-pinched world would not love that?

One person who would: this penny-pinched writer who's always on the lookout for that next check.

Yes, I'm in absolute awe of this ability to give an enormous middle finger to the people in charge of this rat race. To just opt out. To know I need not bow down to any man, woman, or dominant rhetoric because I have the equivalent of a money press in my own two hands. But this very capitalistic validation of one's success, this thumbs-up from the very market forces one claims to despise, it feels to me the most crass and fallible measure of success possible. Is this art, these so-called transgressive, felonious gestures? Or are they not just ornaments in the palaces of our aristocrats?

But then again, that escape is so compelling, that image of a person who can just be himself without having to compromise. I crave that authenticity.

Except, except, what Banksy does isn't politics exactly, it's not street fighting, this man isn't eating pepper spray and hurling tear gas back into the faces of the riot police. For want of a better word, he is called an *artist*.

But is it art?

Well it certainly sells like art. After Banksy kick-started the land grab in street art, his auction prices hurtled toward the hundreds of thousands of dollars. Even though he doesn't get any of that money, he does get the profits from his prints, which he sells to his fans at a tenth of the price they receive on eBay. He could be a lot wealthier than he is—he could jack his prices, he could finally accept Nike's offers to design for them, he could go on a speaking tour and get $100,000 a lecture. He doesn't do any of these things. And, honestly, I don't besmirch him any of his wealth, because he's not the kind of guy who goes out and buys six-packs of Rolexes that come with their own custom-made wrists that agitate them so that their intricate mechanisms won't stop working while they sit in the closet of your mansion. No, what he does is, he takes his money and plows it back into an anti-Disneyland in the British countryside, one of his biggest and most successful pieces post–*Exit Through the Gift Shop*. He calls it Dismaland, he fills it with outstanding art, and he lets people in for £3. Those who end up visiting are the kinds of people who have never visited an art museum in their lives. And then after he's done, he tears it down and donates the spare parts to build refugee shelters. Or he goes back home to Bristol, he puts on the most elaborate, most popular show the Bristol Museum has ever seen, and he pays with his own money so they can give free admission.

And perhaps this is why I can't help but like Banksy. Because after all of these years, after this inordinate, life-changing success, after his public persona has probably eaten up all but some puny vestige of whoever Banksy originally was—after all of this, he still retains enough of his punk aesthetic to keep making things that give me the lulz.

Run the Jewels: "We the hooligans outside of school again, Sayin don't be a fool never follow rules again, We the bad boys bully with the fully that, The teachers say ain't shit and in the need of discipline, We the goddamn reason for Ritalin, In the back of the class, twitchin' and fidgetin' "

Inevitably, Banksy and Thierry meet. Thierry just happens to be available right when Banksy comes to LA for that first-ever U.S. show with the painted elephant. So Thierry shows him around, takes him to all the best walls. And what a serendipitous pairing! Banksy immediately realizes that Thierry is exactly what he's been waiting for. He's the unblinking eyeball that will follow him around and record everything.

That's what Banksy tells us from beneath his gigantic hoodie, and I'm going to call bullshit here, because Banksy has already got a crew. He's got plenty of people to help him build elaborate pieces of art, cart them around, and drop them off. He has also got people who filmed him in the Tate and the West Bank. Banksy may have seen something in Thierry, but it wasn't his camera.

But anyway, Banksy and Thierry bond over some stunts in LA, they hang out in the UK and become true bros, and now we at last seem to be getting to the point of this film: "the incredible true story of how the greatest graffiti movie of all time was never made . . ." Banksy tells Thierry the time has come to take all this film he's been recording for years and turn it into the definitive narrative of the street art movement. So Thierry gets to work. He goes home, he sorts through his thousands of VHS cassettes, he loads it all into Final Cut Pro. He works and works and works. At last he has a film ready for Banksy's two eyes. He shows it to him, and . . . it's utter crap. The very worst crap imaginable. In the words of Banksy: "It was at that point I realized that maybe Thierry wasn't a filmmaker, he was maybe just someone with mental problems who happened to have a camera. It just seemed to go on and on. It was an hour and a half of unwatchable nightmare trailer, essentially like someone with a short attention span and with a remote control flicking through a cable box of nine hundred channels."

This should be the end of the film. The greatest graffiti movie of all time never got made because Thierry's a man-child with the cinematic skills of a teenager clutching a selfie stick. But things don't end here. Banksy decides he's going to take a crack at putting together this documentary, and to distract Thierry for a while he suggests he might make some of his own art.

How curious. Banksy just tells him, go run along now and make some art. Thierry goes back to LA, and he proceeds to do what can only be described as mass produce street art merchandise. He hires a bunch of out-of-work, post-MFA art school kids, he fills a gigantic warehouse deep in the wilds of Los Angeles with these charming Millennials, and then he proceeds to spew out at them an unending stream of kitschy craft projects. Shakespeare with the word "GRAFFITI" stamped on his forehead. The Mona Lisa turned into a barcode. A gigantic robot made out of old TV sets. Elvis Presley cradling an assault rifle instead of a guitar. Leonard Nimoy with Marilyn Monroe hair. Larry King with Marilyn Monroe hair. Jack Nicholson with Marilyn Monroe hair.

At some point in this process he starts calling himself Mr. Brainwash. "I came up with the idea that the whole movement of art is all about brainwashing. OBEY is about brainwashing, Banksy is about brainwashing, so I used MBW, and I am *Mister Brainwash*."

With an absolutely straight face he compares his working method to Damien Hirst's.

I have to say, on some days it seems the modern art world is all about nerve. Hirst got his big break after exhibiting a work made of maggots consuming a cow's head. When his career-defining piece—an actual dead shark encased in a tank—was critiqued on the grounds that anyone could have done it, his inevitable reply was, "But you didn't, did you?" And if nerve really is the necessary ingredient of any mega-successful contemporary artist, well, Thierry has got that. He may have nothing else except nerve.

I don't think it would be too much of a stretch to say that MBW's art is basically Photoshopping images that are so ubiquitous in our media environment it's impossible you don't have at least a trace amount of them in your head. Images as familiar as Darth Vader's grim-faced mask. He takes those images and he just kind of crayons over them.

Thierry's art is a little like these tidbits that I've enjoyed at the San Francisco MOMA museum café. They've managed to create little slices of cake that look like Wayne Thiebaud slices of cake, and little pastries that look like Mondrian canvases. Cute shit like that. And after a long, hard afternoon of looking at real art, I retreat to the café and see all these edible replicas staring me in the face, and I can't help but think, *how clever!* and *oh, so pretty!* and then I buy one and gobble it down my throat. In their shelf-life, their recipe-level mass production, their blatant plagiarism, and their literal-minded transparency, those snacks are essentially indistinguishable from MBW's contribution to the world of art.

Vanessa Place and Robert Fitterman: "Note that in post-conceptual work, there is no distinction between manipulation and production, object and sign, contemplation and consumption. Interactivity has been proved as potentially banal as a Disney cruise, active as a Pavlovian dinner bell."

MBW is the curse of Andy Warhol come to punish us for our sins. Warhol initiated the era of mass conceptualism, and ever since that day art has become divorced from a mastery of technique. You don't need any particular artistic skills to make conceptual art, you just need an idea and some leftover detritus from the capitalist world. Anybody can do it. Which is wonderful, because it democratizes the art world, and it opens up the whole category of "art" to things no one would have imagined. But this is also terrible, because Warhol's own success means that nowadays he looks obvious, and his audacity has been replaced by ubiquity. Right at this second, thousands of art students are making their own Marilyn Monroe silkscreen—which is a great case-study in what late capitalist culture does to audacious artistic gestures: what was upsetting twenty years ago is now regarded by most everyone as conventional. Yesterday's "Piss Christ" is today's kitsch keychain. In a single generation, shock becomes obviousness, and cultural amnesia comes in to trick the small-minded into believing that the original innovation was easy.

So it is with Banksy and his ilk: what was a felony-level activity just twenty years ago is now virtually a national treasure—

in 2017 much of Banksy's remaining street art is protected by sheets of perspex. And Thierry is precisely the sort of person to believe that swooping in and latching on to the innovation Banksy et al. fought for is tantamount to doing what they have done: discovering something that feels vital and raw years before the culture at large knows it and having the determination to keep at it while everyone else regards you as an idiot.

And I think this gets to the heart of my mixed feelings about Banksy: his success is only possible because the culture has caught up to him. His cutting-edge gesture has become something professors teach. And ever since then he's been commoditizing his own innovation. Which makes me uneasy, because I believe the artist's path should always be back toward that cutting edge, that if the market validates what you do, it's probably an indication that it's time to move on.

Thierry may be devoid of anything that's required to make actual art, save nerve, but something of Banksy has rubbed off onto him. Namely, Banksy's intense capacity to leverage the mass media edifice for his own glorification. MBW is doing this same thing, except, instead of leveraging, say, the Palestinian cause, he's leveraging the accumulated credibility of the street art movement. And, let's be honest, the street art movement had already done a pretty good job of leveraging its own credibility by the time Thierry got there. So what MBW is doing begins to look like some kind of toxic, collateralized, real estate derivative that's being passed around from banker to banker like a social disease. All the good land has already been grabbed, all the people who bought a Banksy for $25 in 1999 have already sold it for one thousand times as much in 2006. That ship has left port, friends, but just over here we have this great new investment offer!

And here's the thing: much as I critique Banksy for doing a magnificent job of promoting himself and his art while looking like he's just a loner trying to do his thing, I think he's still a smart, self-made, ballsy guy. He can mortgage his credibility to the hilt because he was the goddamned one to make it in the first place. MBW on the other hand … he's basically writing bad checks on Banksy's cultural currency.

And this is capitalism in a nutshell: reified spectacle, consumable in individual portions for one small cash payment.

This is how art becomes capital.

Adorno: "What parades as progress in the culture industry, as the incessantly new which it offers us, remains the disguise for an eternal sameness; everywhere the changes mask a skeleton which has changed just as little as the profit motive."

So MBW has his small army of post-MFA Millennials churn out an industrial amount of faux street art, and he takes all that merch and convenes the grandest exhibition of Brainwash-related goods the world has ever seen. If Banksy will do an LA show with one hundred pieces, MBW will do one with ten thousand. Outside of major cultural institutions, no one has ever seen an art exhibit of this scope. He's mortgaging every last asset he owns in order to produce more and more Mr. Brainwash product, and he's stuffing it all into over 125,000 square feet of abandoned office space.

He writes to Banksy to tell him all about the show, and Banksy gives him a bemused little blurb that he blows up to the size of a school bus and sticks on the side of his building. Fairey writes him a press release on his personal website, which MBW somehow spins into an *LA Weekly* cover story.

MBW hypes and hypes and hypes, and before you know it he sells nearly a million dollars' worth of merch on his opening weekend. The "Life Is Beautiful" show runs for three months and pulls in 50,000 visitors. He pulls this off in the summer of 2008, mere weeks before the collapse of Lehman Brothers, which takes the entire art market down with it.

It's the ultimate street art dare, and Thierry has won it. Forget walking into the Tate Britain and sticking a canvas up on the wall, Thierry has taken out hundreds of thousands of dollars in credit. He's a middle-aged man with a family and a reasonably comfortable standard of living. Sure, his art is crap, but, ultimately, even if Thierry's art is a bunch of commoditized, overly clever, massed-produced, kitschy garbage, the fact of what he just pulled off is very, very real.

That is, if this isn't all bullshit.

For if there's one message that Banksy's art hammers home more than any other, it's this: don't believe what you see. A world of authority projected through the mass media is a world of images where power isn't based in who a person really is but in who's their avatar on a screen. It's a world of manufactured spectacles designed to convince the free citizens of democratized societies to accept the power structure that's in place. And we can never lose sight of the fact that the person who has created this film is a master of this spectacle.

And you have to ask: who was it that took all this footage of Thierry putting his show together? Answer: Banksy's people filmed him. And who were these "few people who might be able to help him out" that Banksy so casually calls when it looks like Thierry's show is going to fall apart? Answer: Daniel Salin, who produced Banksy's "Barely Legal" show in LA, and Roger Gastman, who in 2011 curated a 40,000 sq ft show in LA's MOCA museum that set a record with over 250,000 attendees.

So what to make of these deadpan, deadly ambiguous reaction shots after MBW's grand success? Quoth Banksy: "There's no one quite like Thierry, even if his art does look quite a lot like everyone else's."

Quoth Fairey: "Even when you have the best intentions sometimes things can go awry."

Banksy: "I always used to encourage everybody I met to make art; I used to think everyone should do it. I don't really do that so much any more."

Slavoj Žižek: "Many viewers find ['Gangnam Style'] disgustingly attractive, i.e., they 'love to hate it,' or, rather, they enjoy finding it disgusting, so they repeatedly play it to prolong their disgust—this compulsive nature of the obscene *jouissance* in all its stupidity is what true art should release us from."

So what exactly is this film, a documentary or a feature?

Let it be known that Theirry isn't just any guy. In 2014, *The New York Observer* confirmed he owned millions of dollars of real estate around LA before he became MBW. He's a powerful landlord, and way back in 2001 he secured a $600,000 line of credit for his fashion ventures, which were quite successful. (Among other things, he blatantly pirated Warner Bros. properties for his clothing lines, but instead of suing him into oblivion Warner Bros. simply licensed what he had made and split the profits.) By comparison, Thierry's 2008 show required just a $320,000 line of credit.

But even if you don't know all that, anyone who makes it to the end of *Exit Through the Gift Shop* has just about the same reaction: What the fuck is going on here? Is Banksy telling us an honest story? Is MBW Banksy's greatest creation, as many people assert, or did MBW play Banksy?

Using game theory, I can see four possible ways to interpret this film. I'm going to start from the bottom, by which I mean the interpretation that assumes the film isn't trying to trick us, and then move up through increasing levels of we're-being-lied-to.

1) Banksy didn't invent MBW, MBW isn't a fake

Banksy really is anguished at what he's helped to bring into the art world, and he's not going to encourage anyone to make art any longer. Sadly, MBW really thinks his work is art, and not only that, he's managed to convince a good deal of the art collecting establishment that his work is art too. The movie is a legit documentary demonstrating that the art world is more crass and depressing than even we believed.

2) Banksy didn't invent MBW, MBW is a fake

Banksy is still anguished, but even worse, MBW has gotten one over on one of the greatest pranksters of the contemporary era. MBW worked his relationship with Banksy and used him. He knows he's just selling commoditized garbage to unsuspecting suckers, and he's not even pretending that there's some larger goal on the artistic agenda. MBW is just cashing in, and he's pulled it off. The art world is so full of enablers and cut-throats that even Banksy got burned.

3) Banksy invented MBW, MBW isn't a fake

All those arch comments Banksy makes down the line are actually perfect deadpans, because MBW is his most elaborate prank ever, and Fairey is probably in on it, too. MBW doesn't realize his artistic existence is in fact an elaborate joke pulled off by his street art godfather. Only the parts of this film in which MBW speaks directly are documentary, and the parts with Banksy, Shepard, et al. are straight-up acting. Given all the screen time Banksy and MBW share—and all the time they were together in real life—this possibility is almost preposterous. How could he have conned MBW so hard? Banksy is one bad mother.

4) Banksy invented MBW, MBW is a fake

Everybody's in on it and this whole film is basically bullshit. In which case, give MBW some kind of an award, because he nails his good-for-nothing, self-aggrandizing-idiot persona. And, given the scope of his career post-film, he's been nailing it ever since; we're talking Banksy-esque levels of public duplicity. Imagine the implications! Banksy just engineered a duplicate that will run around spreading his aesthetic and further bankrolling his empire. His is the goddamn chess master.

As to the truth?

In its purest sense art isn't about managing a career or pursuing some grand ambition, it's about doing a thing that you have no choice but to submit to. By definition, it's contrary to scheming and duplicity. All artists start here, and *Exit Through the Gift Shop* is about people who came to their art for precisely that reason. But a life must have a trajectory, an artist must find a profession.

Which is to say, I think in the beginning Fairey wanted a friend who would go out bombing with him and film him doing his thing. And I think Banksy trusted Fairey; when he came to LA he needed a guy, and when he eventually realized whom he was dealing with, he weighed the pros and the cons and made a choice. And Thierry, like so many of us, was impressed by Banksy's mystique, was thrilled to be breathing the same air as this man and seeing what his face actually looked like.

But as the saying goes, familiarity breeds contempt, and as so awe turned to avarice. And maybe Banksy wanted to give that avarice a little push. Maybe out of pique, and maybe also because he thought it would make a great story.

Like all things in life, art is a social phenomenon, we are social creatures. No matter how many times Banksy has said people should leave his street art to decay and be painted over, the fact is he doesn't completely believe this. He wanted someone to record his doings. He wanted it to last. After all, he himself admits that the Internet is what made street art a true movement—it gave graffiti a second, permanent life online and let millions discover it.

Even though art only really requires us and our canvas, we crave interpretation. Few of us will be satisfied to just make a piece and let it molder unseen. When I feel the thrill of an idea materializing on the page, I want it to be read. I don't care about money or fame or anything like that, I just want someone to connect with what I've done. And I can't believe Banksy feels any different when he's in the ecstasy of bombing. That's the tension: art should need nothing more than fulfilling that mandate to create, but it seems this isn't enough. So we bring in others, we lose control of what was once ours. From this compromise arises aesthetics and morality.

This contamination makes art immensely more complex and interesting than it would have been otherwise. It creates questions of authenticity and authority. It makes us worry over our engagement with the market. It sharpens us with doubt.

By giving himself an other, Banksy has made his own art immensely more interesting. Thierry has forced him to stare into the contradictions that would never have materialized had he remained a self-satisfied lone wolf spraying sarcastic gestures onto walls and then walking away. The result was his most substantial piece yet: this film, this man.

And so perhaps this is my peace with the vulgar market, that dreaded need to earn when I would just rather create. One must have contradictions, or all this drive to make is nothing more than a drive to push against a void. One requires a wall.

2015, IN MEDIAS RES
Boyhood, Richard Linklater (2014)

They say agriculture was the original sin.

Twelve-thousand years ago humans began to farm. The baggyness of hunting and gathering was giving way to the fixity of settlements. Populations grew. We became too numerous to return to the old ways.

Civilization had begun, and writing was needed. It was imperative to know who had what, who was owed, who was owned. Chieftains amassed vast wealth and power, they found that the markings they used to track their empires could be repurposed to codify rules for living. They began to record their doings and their decrees. Law and history thus came into being. Society now had a memory that would outlast the life of any human.

The narratives that dominate our world found a fixed existence beyond the limits of the oral tradition. They could be disseminated far and wide, and they would live not a mere 80 years but so long as their parchment survived. With the help of these master discourses, the children of kings were taught to be kings, the children of slaves were told they're slaves. Power invented ever better justifications for its rule. The shape of things grew steadier by the day.

The tides of history rage, always premised on these first, insurmountable tales. But still there are those whose will is to repudiate them. Our histories honor those who have defied them in spectacular fashion: their names will come easily to the tongue, they are known today in our holidays, our myths and legends, our most hallowed books. They reach us from a million points of the social fabric, as do the histories written by their fellows in arms and those who crushed them.

Stories atop stories atop stories. For thousands of years it has been this way.

Here we are now, a world full of its own inevitability.

Which brings me to Richard Linklater. A man who makes films about the ways we're guided to where we're supposed to be in this enormous collective tale called history. Normally Linklater's movies examine just one small part of this process—for instance, how a few summer days of bullying and sex situate adolescents into a hierarchy—but with his seventeenth film he managed to fit *twelve years' worth* of social conditioning into an epic three hours. From first-grader to college student, how the social fabric claims us. A boyhood.

André Breton: "It is perhaps childhood that comes closest to one's 'real life.'"

It starts in Mason's sixth year on planet Earth. His mother is collecting him after school, and she's exasperated because the boy fails to turn in his homework. *You just have to turn it in!* The child doesn't get it. He's done the homework, he's learned the lesson—why does he have to turn it in too? It's pointless. Olivia is almost screaming. *It doesn't make any difference! You just have to because you just have to!*

There's a reason why Linklater puts this scene first. It's played out a million times in any childhood, this incessant cramming of rules for living.

Olivia is the sort of person who feels safety in her spot on the social order. It frightens her to be out on a limb, not knowing what she's doing and where she's headed. When the movie starts she's divorced and seeking a man to be a proper father to Mason and his sister. She wants a nice secure house with enough room for everyone, family dinners, wholesome vacations. If it's not too much, a tidy little career for herself, too.

One night she's arguing with her current boyfriend, because he's been out having fun while she's been taking care of her kids. He asks Olivia: Why don't you just go out and have a drink with us? That innocent little question unleashes a shitstorm. She screams back that she *would just love* to go to a bar. She *wishes to god* she could just go to a *fucking bar* and have a *fucking beer* and not worry about any responsibilities for just one night. *First I was somebody's daughter,* she screams, *then I was somebody's mother. I don't know what that's fucking like!*

That's Olivia: always somebody's something. Her whole life has been figuring out who the people around her need her to be. And she's enraged because she didn't exactly want this life, but she knows she's going to keep doing it.

Through the walls of his room Mason can hear the muffled yells of Olivia and her boyfriend. This clearly isn't the first time he's lain in bed listening to his mother rage, and these fights have scarred him. Be that as it may, he still doesn't have the slightest idea what it's all about. Childhood is when you don't yet know you have to serve somebody. You don't get it. That's precisely what it is to grow up. You assume all the rights, responsibilities, and cognitions of a full-fledged human being. And in return you spend the rest of your life yearning for that childhood innocence before you understood you have to serve somebody.

Serving somebody isn't that bad. Sure, you've got to punch a clock, you've got to pay attention to pointless little details, you've got to flatter the boss's intelligence. Those are the compromises you make to be an adult. And here's the rub: when you're a child you haven't been granted the freedom to make those compromises. As you earn the freedom to make your compromises, you become adult.

So masochistic, the way we're made to participate in our own domestication. But that's the trade. And who really wants that ignorance back? Who would give up sex and alcohol and the possibility of contemplating questions so large they'll squash you?

But when you're six you know nothing at all of this, you have no idea why mom is screaming at her boyfriend that she would *just love* to do exactly what she wanted for once in her life. And nor do you understand why, the next morning, your older sister is in full brat mode, waking you up with a stuffed animal to the head and belting out Britney Spears's "Oops! I Did It Again." Not only is Samantha singing just like Britney Spears, she's dancing like her too, shaking her childish hips, flinging her tiny hands through her hair. It's clear she has no idea what these moves are. She doesn't know that when Britney shakes her hips and spreads her hair, teenage boys get hard-ons. She and her brother are just innocent little children copying whatever they see on television.

Robert Bresson: "Nine-tenths of our movements obey habit and automatism."

As Samantha cavorts and sings, Mason screams *stop it!*, but then once mom runs in, Samantha suddenly transforms. She's crying, *Mason is bullying me!* It's an amazing performance, but it's also perfectly ordnary. We are all consummate actors. It's a part of human nature, a thing we do so automatically that we barely ever realize we spend our whole lives acting like ourselves.

Olivia decides that to raise her children without ending up in the poor house she needs to go back to school, so she moves the family in with her mother. While Sam and Mason spend their days with grandma, Olivia sits in a classroom and studies. We see exactly one of Olivia's student classes. It's one of the most important scenes in the film.

Behind the lectern is Professor Bill, a teddy bear sort with a paunch and gray hair, and he's telling the class about Pavlov's dog. This is the essence of conditioning, he says. Ring a bell every time you bring a dog its food, and pretty soon the dog will salivate when it hears that chime. It's right like that first scene with Mason, when Olivia's screaming at him to just turn in his stupid homework: Do something we like and you get a pat. Do something we don't like and you get a smack. Every day, a thousand smacks and a thousand pats. Pretty soon all you need to do is think about something and you feel that hand.

Rilke: "If no one else, the dying / must notice how unreal, how full of pretence, / is all that we accomplish here, where nothing / is allowed to be itself."

Professor Bill starts with conditioning, but then he swerves—from the ringing bell that makes the dog drool to the saliva whose origins are mysterious. Why does the smell of meat produce saliva? What exactly happens in the brain? Nobody knows. Professor Bill calls it an *unlearned, involuntary, unconditioned* response. Unlearned. Involuntary. Unconditioned. This is saliva. No one tells you to salivate, and you can't stop it happening. The condition of every infant. Our state before civilization gets its hooks into us. Unlearned, involuntary, unconditioned.

What's another unlearned, involuntary, unconditioned response? asks Professor Bill. *Some of you are probably experiencing it right now.*

Sexual arousal.

Things get quite complicated when we love someone we shouldn't, or when we're forced to love someone we don't. The world would be a lot simpler if we could fake love, if we could just turn it off when it's inconvenient, but love is implacable. And this is why the social order fears love—it knows love can break it. It knows it can't be stopped. So love gets hidden behind layers of shame and mystery and morality.

If you watch enough of Linklater's films, eventually you realize that love occupies a special place in his conception of the world. It's a universal solvent for breaking apart the things we're instructed to believe. Love opens up little bits of space for freedom. It clears away just enough of that smacking and patting that's been filling your brain since Day 1 for you to decide what you want. Think of Romeo and Juliet, a classic case. They're willing to ignore their social codes, their blood vendettas, even their families, all because of love. Bad idea. They let love guide them, and in the end society destroys them for it.

Maybe this is why Linklater's films always cut me so deep. Look at Romeo and Juliet again. If they had done as they were told, nobody would remember them. Shakespeare wouldn't have told their story, and you wouldn't be forced to read it in high school. It's the tales of love versus society that make for the strongest emotions. That's why these stories become timeless. And that's why this film feels so powerful to me. On the surface, *Boyhood* may look like a bunch of average people learning to follow the rules, but it's really about that little voice of love, and what you learn to do with it.

But to return to Professor Bill's lecture on arousal. It turns out the old cad wasn't merely speculating when he said that *some of you may be feeling it right now.* As the students shuffle out from the lecture hall, Olivia sticks around to introduce Professor Bill to her little Mason, and right away teacher starts hitting on student. The months rush by, and just like that they're married! Olivia moves in. She has a family again. A house, beautiful children, a loving spouse, the cusp of a career. The perfect suburban dream! But of course Richard Linklater has other plans for her.

Before we get to that, let me tell you about another lecture, one that happens about five years after the Pavlovian one. This lecture is its natural rhyme. Now Olivia's the professor—she's earned her Ph.D., and she's giving her students her own take on love. She says that human survival depends on us falling in love. Not the mature, sexual love that Professor Bill brought up, the love between mother and child. Olivia's theory says that love is the only explanation for why a mother would risk her life to protect her babies. Evolution taught us to love our children as a survival mechanism.

By implication, the love you feel for your partner, I mean the tender love that forms the bedrock of a lifelong romantic relationship, that love is just you repurposing what evolution built to be used on your children. And society tries to repurpose it too.

It tries to harness that love into a duty that keeps us productive, stable, in check. I understand this, and I respect it, and I have my own loves that I try to balance on that narrow point between duty and passion. As you age, life has a way of being more and more heavy-handed in turning your passion to a duty, so with every 24 hours that balance gets a little harder to sustain. But I need it, I need it to keep that passion large and sustain this little space I've carved for myself.

Speaking of careful balances, I first watched *Boyhood* while propped aloft against the Earth's atmosphere and hurtling between North America and Europe. I would need to be a specialist to explain all the laws and treaties governing my body during those twelve airborne hours, the airspaces and jurisdictions and legalities I passed through. I only know that they are very different from the laws that acted upon me the day I first wedged myself into the seat of a jetliner in 1995. When I'm in the airport, I perform the required activities as though they have always been so, perpetrating a sort of mass amnesia. Whoever has legislated these demands upon my body is all powerful, they cannot be trifled with. Who can help but be awed at this demonstration of how we humans create order from chaos?

How much lighter might the law have sat upon me were I born twenty years earlier? I'll never know. The law does not live and die as we do. It is deathless. It grows and grows and grows. Our mortality is its trump, and against it we play love. Law and love, two old antagonists, their struggles never ceasing, their friction giving heat to our lives.

Derrida: "It seems that the law should never give rise to any story. To be invested with its categorical authority, the law must be without history, genesis, or any possible derivation."

The psychology professors are in love. They marry. It's precisely when Professor Bill and Olivia return from their honeymoon in Paris that I begin to notice an extraordinary technique of Linklater's that has thus far flown under the radar. The couple's four children are playing on a trampoline in the back yard, and there's Sam in a pink shirt, still running around like a little girl, except now she's developing. Her step-sister is too.

Adolescence gives *Boyhood* its distinct texture. Linklater did something that has never been done before in film: he made this movie over 12 years, shooting a handful of scenes each year, syncing them up with the characters' on-screen age. So when Ellar Coltrane's character Mason Jr. is 8 years old, Ellar Coltrane is 8. And when Mason Jr. is 14, Coltrane is 14. This is how it works for everyone. By the time Samantha is reaching adolescence, I would guess that we're probably in year 4 of *Boyhood's* decade-plus odyssey. Sam's body is changing in a way I've never, ever seen a body change in a film. Half an hour ago she was a little girl miming Britney Spears, and now she's becoming a teenager. And so is Mason. Olivia's moving toward middle age. They're all four years older.

A year later some older boy is showing Mason and his stepbrother how to look up pornography on the Internet. It's a typical rite of boyhood, you and your friends staring through shame and awe at the sexualized breasts of a full-grown woman. Suddenly the door flies open and in walks Mason's stepsister, still at that in-between age when her body is much more mature than her mind. As the boys shamefacedly hide the computer, they can't help but stare at her t-shirt, which is much too tight. This scene is so perfect in its confusion, its mixed messages and crossed desires. That is what the fabric of this film achieves, the sensation of struggling through the confusion as you work through your childhood.

Speaking of struggling to grow up: a couple years before this moment, right after Olivia moved back in with her mother and decided to return to school—that is, when Professor Bill and his children are still just dots on the horizon—Sam and Mason's father comes back into the picture. It's not exactly clear why Olivia and Mason Sr. called it quits, but we're given to understand that it has something to do with Olivia being a bit of a wet blanket and Mason Sr. a bit of a screw-up. They're obviously two people going in completely different directions. But now he's right there on grandma's porch, an overgrown adolescent stuffing his kids into the back of his seatbeltless Pontiac GTO and taking them to the bowling alley. So they go, they bowl, it's great, and right there in the middle of that kindly old temple of suburban family fun there's a big-screen TV showing the bodies of four Blackwater mercenary soldiers being dragged through the streets of Fallujah. Mason Sr. decides to use this as an impromptu opportunity to lecture his children on the evils of the Bush Administration. And this is all so apt, the way you can be having a day at the bowling alley, just another blissful childhood afternoon chugging Coca-Cola and throwing strikes, when all of a sudden a TV screen displays one of the most chilling images of your entire childhood, all the people around you throwing strikes and living their lives. This is just the way it happens. We live our entire childhood in this sea of 24-hour media. Who knows, maybe when he's 25 years old Mason Jr. will awake from a deep sleep with the foggy memory of the mercenaries, and he'll spend a second wondering just what that afternoon was. I myself will never forget my childish views of the white Bronco bearing OJ Simpson away from the LAPD, the rioter who delivered a flying kick to Reginald Denny's skull, the First Gulf War—these televised spectacles that I could not help being impressed by, even though I had no real idea what they were, the massive master narratives they were serving. Mason Sr. is trying to clue his children into these narratives in his own way, one of the things the older generation must do for the younger.

Following that afternoon, Mason Sr. keeps drifting back into his children's lives, while Olivia is meeting Professor Bill and beginning her second marriage. It starts out great but soon begins to sour. Contrary to his sweet, gently authoritative posture in the classroom, it turns out that Professor Bill is actually an extraordinarily awful husband and father. To be perfectly blunt, he's an alcoholic, dictatorial asshole who crops off all Mason's "girly" hair, treats the kids like chattel, and eventually begins smacking Olivia.

While Professor Bill is turning the household into *1984*, Mason Sr.'s parenting is more like *Lord of the Flies*. He has the kids on weekends for sleepovers in his disheveled little apartment. One night, father and son are lying down to sleep next to each other, and Jr. asks Sr. if there's such a thing as magic. It's dark, they're alone, and he's frightened, he just wants his dad to reassure him that nothing freaky is going to come and get him in the night. But Sr. can't stomach the idea of such a prosaic world. So instead of reassuring Jr. he rebuts him. Of course magic exists! If you'd never heard of a whale before and I described it to you, wouldn't that seem magical? For Jr., there's far too much chaos out there in the world, and he'd like to reign it in a little; but Sr.'s world feels far too orderly, and he's desperate to convince himself that life isn't quite so boring.

When is it that we become adult? When I was younger I would have told you the answer was age 22, the year I graduated college and fell in love, when I'd consolidated my rights as a United States citizen and was forced to earn a living. But now that I'm older, I think I'd tell you the answer is at least 35, because in those 13 intervening years I came to see lines that were once invisible, I saw how I'd connected the threads of my identity, how my life couldn't help but resolve itself into narrative. I found that the world really will impose itself on you, I'd seen the stakes, understood what was over with for good, what was left to fight for, how difficult the last battles would be, where I could compromise, where I could not. I'd learned that all of this was to be the foundation for the second half of my life—the final half of my life. I felt the weight of that first half and knew that it was immovable.

After one final, alcohol-fueled disaster, Olivia ditches Professor Bill, calls child protective services on what remains of his household, gets a new place to live, a new boyfriend. Now Mason is a full-fledged adolescent, and he's on a sleepover. When you're the child of modestly middle-class parents and feel secure in your place, you begin to do things for no other reason than that they sound fun and might be a little dangerous. So it is that one night Mason finds himself "camping" in a partially constructed house with some older boys, hurling a buzzsaw blade the size of his skull at a plywood board, drinking beers, and pretending that a stripper is about to drop in. This is the scene Linklater puts exactly at *Boyhood's* halfway point, a scene that always seems just on the verge of going somewhere in a movie that always seems just on the verge of going somewhere. That sawblade, what if there's an accident? Is this adolescent energy going to boil over into something sinister? Is a woman really headed over there? This scene is absolutely saturated with potential, but it never becomes anything more than a bunch of kids killing a Friday night, just one of countless childhood Fridays that must be slaughtered. I can still remember those nights before my life's narrative took shape, but I can no longer remember how it felt to be so far from being someone, just piling up incident after incident with no particular coherence. It's only once you've understood where you fit into the world-governing narratives that you're capable of turning your life into a story. You have to be taught the ideology of it, to learn to recognize the little turning points and milestones that are supposed to make us adult humans. I have been taught this ideology, and that's why, as I watch Richard Linklater's movie, I keep wanting the scene with the sawblade to go somewhere, because I've been conditioned, I need it to resolve into some sort of significance. My ideas of adolescence and film tell me that a scene like this has to go somewhere. But Linklater never takes it anywhere. Mason and his friends keep throwing the sawblade, nobody gets hurt, they keep drinking the beers and playing childish games to establish their pecking order. I understand that this is Linklater showing me how I've been taught to salivate like Pavlov's dog when I see a life-moment arcing toward meaning—my mind just completes it. I kept feeling chills run down my spine in my Boeing 747 seat, despite the fact that nothing in particular ever happens in this movie—no tragedy, no triumph, no revelation, no conclusion—and I even felt some thick tears at the scene with the sawblade and haven't ever found a way to escape it.

While I'm on the subject of mile-high screenings, I should acknowledge the fact that watching an in-flight movie is a very strange thing. A few years before I made my mid-air, midnight, red-eye viewing of *Boyhood*, Virgin Atlantic conducted a survey that found over half its passengers admitting "heightened emotions" while flying. Forty-one percent of men said they hid in-flight tears. Soon followed a fad of true confessions about crying at the in-flight movie, then a raft of theories about why we're so emotional on a plane. To me this is a classic question of conditioning versus free will: is it that we're made to think of flying as a high-stakes, high-pressure, dangerous experience, or is it the natural consequence of being crammed through layers of security, stuffed into controlled, low-oxygen environments, and fed mediocre food? Who knows. I have always felt emotional before and during flights. I am filled with relief once I have landed and cleared the airport. I have no doubts whatsoever about the statistics showing that you are far more likely to die by shark attack, lightning strike, or bee sting than on a flight, but nevertheless, flights, without fail, focus my mind on the fact of my death. I well remember the movies I see on them. These movies are bound to bizarre, intense emotions that make them unique in my mind.

Hélène Cixous: "What is outside of us during the day takes place in us during the night."

Shortly after the sawblade sleepover, Mason is turning 15. He's sliding out the rear window of a hatchback, toking and necking with a beautiful young woman. I like Mason as a teenager. He has long droopy hair, wears tight, battered jeans, and paints his fingernails. He speaks with a shy lethargy in a deepening voice. He is capable of embracing that rare moment when you can smoke and neck and drink with little to no consequences, no worries about tomorrow as you slide up to your mother's house well past midnight. When Mason makes it inside, we see that Olivia has thrown a party—she's still young yet!—and there's husband number three asking Mason, *do you know what time it is?* And because this film has been conditioning me so well, I expect husband number three to bark out, *it's you're-goddamned-late-o'clock and your mother's so worried!*, but he doesn't say that, he just says it's past midnight, which means you're a year older now. That's it, another Linklater anticlimax reminding me how much I need things to happen in stories.

The next morning Mason and Samantha are heading out in Mason Sr.'s minivan—yes, he's sold off his sexy little Pontiac for a dadmobile—and as they drive to their grandparents-in-law Sam is showing Sr.'s new wife Lady Gaga on her smartphone, and Sr. is introducing Jr. to a special mix he's made for him of all the Beatles' solo albums. It's the early 2010s, they have all effortlessly mastered the technologies of portable, sortable pop culture. *There's this decade of music that's been scattered* says Sr., showing Jr. his Beatles mix CD, *and now it's been carefully arranged for you by your father.* Whereas he might have once just explained to his son about how the Beatles didn't really hit their stride as a group until they broke up, now he can document and prove it with a homemade 2-CD set that he slips into his son's hand, complete with custom liner notes. At that moment, building your own mix CD was the height of mainstream chic, but of course this feels a tad bit *quaint* now, because in a year or two Sr. will trade in his mix CDs for a USB cord, and a couple years after that he'll just put it in the cloud or stream Spotify, and not too long after this essay is published even the cloud will look old school. The point is this: the technology changes, but it's still father and son bonding over some tidbit of pop culture they can both manage to relate to.

At grandma and grandpa's Mason gets birthday gifts that could not be a bigger contrast to the Beatles mix CD: a bible, an antique shotgun handed down for generations, and some grown-up interview clothes. Sr. hands his son the shirt and tie almost apologetically, explaining, *you gotta have this, you need it, you've got a whole life ahead of you.*

Necktie, shotgun, bible—work, protection, faith. Evergreens that don't change with the times, no matter what we find to store our music on. The bedrock of culture. When they start bringing these our for you, you know things are getting serious. Society is signing you up for that adult identity you never knew you wanted.

Case in point: when we next see Mason Jr. he's with the grandparents in church, ill-at-ease in his new clothes and confused by the sermon. The priest is talking about Doubting Thomas, who wouldn't believe Jesus had been resurrected until he could poke his fingers through the stigmata. *Blessed are those who can believe without seeing*, the priest observes. I love how he nails his role, he talks about Jesus like he's a chum he sees from time to time, it's exactly the folksy, down-to-earth thing you'd expect from a preacher in a thimble-sized church in rural Texas. His congregation is a bunch of middle-aged believers who have probably lived here their whole lives and heard it all a million times before. There's no need for fire and brimstone and Charlton Heston parting the Red Sea, this priest just says, *blessed are those who believe*, and everyone nods because they know he's right. And he *is* right. Those who believe *are* blessed, because that's the only thing holding together religion. It's the only thing holding civilization together, too. All of us just believing in a bunch of stuff that doesn't exactly exist and can't ever be proven. That's how we keep the world working. Adults know that you just have to believe, but Mason wants to see all these things before he believes in them. Any teenager would. It's human nature. It takes a whole lot of work before you get to the point where you nod sagely when the priest says, *blessed are those who believe.*

The path from seeing to believing, that's the line from Mason Jr. to Mason Sr.

Back at home Olivia is on eBay selling all the junk in her oversized house. It's a desperate attempt to pay off her mortgage, and she's just about cracked. *I spent the first half of my life acquiring all this crap,* she deadpans, *and now I'm going to spend the second half of my life getting rid of it.* Unimpeachable logic! Home ownership, debt, the consumer lifestyle—they're all just more ways to tie you into a story that's not yours. And when I see what Olivia's become, I can't help but think back to the slightly younger Olivia, screaming at her boyfriend that she'd *just fucking love* to know what it was like to do whatever she wants. She still has no idea what that's like! The only difference is, now she *knows* she never will, she knows that her chance to live irresponsibly is long gone, she's accepted that fact, so she's not screaming any more, she's not struggling, she's just chuckling with a little rue and asking Mason to make sure he washes his dish.

Basically my mom is still just as fucking confused as I am, says Mason to his friend.

What attracts Mason to this pretty young woman he meets one night after the football game? They're off secluded while the rest of the party churns distantly, and of course they become attached, and before you know it they're taking a trip to see Sam, who's now a college student in Austin. Driving to another city to spend the weekend away from parental supervision—this is it, their first real taste of childhood's end, the big prelude to the enormous break. *By next summer this will just be our lives* they say to each other, and it's so ironic. They're giddy happy to be sitting in a depressing chain diner eating stale tortilla chips and microwaved cheese at 3:00 in the morning—a few years after college this *will* be their lives, and once again they'll be desperate to escape to a more exciting life. That's childhood—escape after escape after escape. When does it stop? When do you cease escaping and find where you're supposed to be?

Czesław Miłosz: "The purpose of poetry is to remind us / how difficult it is to remain just one person."

As Mason and Sheena begin to look toward adulthood, boy tells girl that their future *is like a pre-ordained slot that's already got your name and number on it.* They joke around about quitting Facebook, about how they can't stop texting their friends to share the things they're still in the process of doing—how texting itself becomes a part of the act, it just slips into every little crevice in your life—and about how, when you think about it, *it's like social networks chemically reward us for letting ourselves be brainwashed.* Mason and Sheena are standard-issue members of their generation. What else would they think when every moment of their childhood has been recorded in precise detail on digital media and stored conveniently in the home? Every moment they've experienced is not only as direct reality but also a second (and third, and fourth . . .) time as mediated reality. Mason and Sheena have in-depth documentation of how they've been watched and instructed all their lives. They've watched as these tools have become more and more invasive, to the point where now it's not just mom and dad constantly recording you, it's everyone, and the very social forces that govern their life force them to participate.

Now there's Mason on the last day of school, some random teacher running into him, and the both of them having to fill the dead air with *something* just to get through the awkward encounter. She offers the following advice: 1) On the moment before he untethers from the nest: *Kinda that voluptuous panic.* 2) On expectations for college: *It's good, it's gonna be crazy good.* 3) On life experiences to come: *You're gonna find your people in college.* 4) On what to do no matter what: *Just follow your heart.* 5) On just because: *Don't forget to floss.*

They're all platitudes, for god's sake, and I'm convinced Linklater threw in that last one just to taunt us! I can see it coming together in Mason's head—he's beginning to realize that the best the adult world can do for him are clichés. Sure, these people have taught him photography, they've taught him math, they've taught him history, science, the English language. They've raised him. But when it comes to actually telling him something that's not on the script . . . *Don't forget to floss.*

There are exceptions. As Mason wastes his fading youth bussing tables at a prefab salad bar, his boss finds him bored, flirting with his coworker, eating some leftover fried shrimp off a used plate. This is unacceptable. Instead of dressing Mason down, his boss encourages him: if he chooses to work hard, a promotion and a raise are possible.

From a certain jaundiced standpoint this is just more of the world prescribing Mason's humanity, but I'm inclined to read it as an act of kindness where people drop the platitudinous bullshit and give you a few moments of memorable honesty. Instead of just pushing Mason along, this man wants to give him a choice. I find this laudable. Regardless of the many platitudes that have undoubtedly formed me, what I remember best from my own youth are those moments when someone found the generosity to open up my vision. These memories can still cut me, make my cheeks redden with shame and my mouth laugh with freedom.

Hélène Cixous: "The message arrives on condition that one does not wait for it, it arrives *unhoped-for, the goal attained unexpectedly.*"

Here I am now, some two hours and thirty minutes after I started, some hundreds of miles closer to Europe, and in a late scene Jr. is asking Sr. what it all means, and dad is replying with more platitudes, *who knows, son, what's important is that you're feeling things.* And now there's Olivia throwing out even more junk while Mason jabbers about how pretty soon they won't even need personality tests to select college roommates, the NSA will just tell you who to go with, and Olivia erupts in fuck-it-all tears at how fast life passes by—isn't everything just a bunch of milestones that someone else told her to cross? And now we've veered sharply to Mason grinding a beat-down Toyota truck through one of those inconceivably gigantic Texas landscapes, arriving at school, his new college roommate giving him pot brownies and taking him to the beautiful rock wilderness with a pretty girl. And now they're getting baked and screaming into the cliffs and asserting that all of creation has unfolded to bring them to this moment, and this is when Mason unreels a little nugget of marijuana wisdom.

It's constant, the moments, it's like it's always right now.

I'm sure that Richard Linklater wouldn't bother with something so anodyne as a capstone moral to a twelve-year project in a film's final line. Mason's just a college freshman who's a little high on weed and giddy at the sight of that young woman smiling at him—what does he know? Linklater's ending *in medias res*, exactly like he began. And as I pull the DVD from its slot on my computer—having now seen *Boyhood* too many times to count—I must reflect that our lives are always *in medias res*. It's all we can do. Spinoza says as much in the *Ethics* when he notes that the further in the future or the past we perceive a thing to be, the less powerfully it affects us. The highest intensity of our experience as human beings is always the 2 to 3 seconds that science has determined constitutes our perception of the present, the only point in time when things are actually occurring. This is what affects us the most.

The eternally fleeting present is a necessary limitation on our experience of life, and it is why we tell stories. The Elysium of our experiences, stories are attempts to imbue the lost past and distant future with the power of the present. Take my sweet ginger feline, who was often nestled by my side as I watched this movie and wrote this essay, generally asleep, perhaps lightly purring or licking himself clean. For ten years I've rubbed this cat's whiskers and watched him doze in sunrays, we've grown older together and watched each other bear up to the weight of thousands more days upon each other's bodies. We have memorized the rhythms of our intersecting lives—these rhythms are what's left over from those innumerable bursts of 2 to 3 seconds that constitute the moments we share. This is how a story works itself into us. Every day, thousands and thousands of bits of experience pattern these rhythms into my mind. These accumulated bits of *in medias res* are what I call on to give shape to my memories. They are the invisible, untouchable shape of our world.

2016, THE MYSTERY (PART II)
Voyage of Time, Terrence Malick (2016)

It was in public school in the 8th grade that I learned the sun is a star on the main sequence. The stellar median, middle-class, milquetoast, not too big, not too small, not too bright, not too dim. Perfectly ordinary.

We were instructed that the sun was halfway through its 10-billion-year main sequence life. It was continually growing brighter and hotter, and once enough time had passed our green and blue planet would find those scorching stellar fires close enough to touch. And then they would engulf the Earth.

Apocalypse. We were bored adolescents being spoken to by a timid woman. I can almost see her face, this kindly person who explained to me the most plausible scenario I have ever heard for how the world will end.

It was in high school that I taught myself the epilogue: the Earth a husk, our solar system unrecognizable, the sun will peaceably collapse into a superdense mass of subatomic matter. A white dwarf. This senile incarnation will last very long: trillions of years, maybe far more. Nobody knows, because the universe itself has scarcely existed a fraction of that duration, so it is impossible to observe what becomes of a white dwarf. Theoretically, should all existence last long enough, the sun will one day complete its life as a chilly, lightless black dwarf.

These are not facts an adolescent is prepared to weigh. The time scale itself was lunacy. Even more lunatic that vision of our cradle immolated. I could not escape the conclusion that whatever humans fled this inferno would be unintelligible to us.

In learning to leave Earth they would have grown strange. This was worse than our annihilation.

What makes us human are the questions that are irresolvable. Our humanity will cease once we learn to render them irrelevant. And yet we strive to do just that. The fate of the Earth disquieted me because it symbolized our profound need to leave ourselves behind.

Heidegger: "'Why are there beings at all instead of nothing?'—this is obviously the first of all questions."

Voyage of Time begins by asking why there is something and not nothing. This is not a question asked by one who means to document science's ideas about the universe. It is the starting point of a director who will use science to ponder mysteries we know we cannot answer. This is the work of the prophet, the poet, the philosopher. Whatever Terrence Malick is, I would call him those things. His films are more like poems of image and sound than straight movie narratives. After working through the questions of love, war, and discovery, he began to ask why the universe exists at all, and what it means that we are in it. He inflated this question to ridiculous proportions in his massive *Tree of Life*, and then he tightened it to an hour in *Voyage of Time*.

Spinoza: "That whose nature involves existence is its own cause, and exists only from the necessity of its nature."

The emergence of being. A quantum fluctuation. A singularity. It breaks outward, it inflates with hideous force. Atoms. All existence is still just a few minutes old. Then ignition, for 17 minutes the entire universe has the character of a single all-encompassing star. Heavier elements form from abundant hydrogen, darkness for hundreds of thousands of years—a literal dark age, the universe is opaque and light cannot move through it. Then gaseous nebulae, the stars igniting and exploding, the universe filling with light—light that is still traveling today, that after passing impossible distances sometimes falls onto mirrors ground by human hands. Complex atoms disperse. More stars from these atoms; more explosions, heavier atoms;

further explosions, even heavier atoms; this for billions of years. Eventually some of those jumbled atoms settle as an ellipse of dust. Planets. An ordinary star.

I have often seen these things. Late at night on the mind's journey toward sleep, weightless in the emptiness of space, kissed by the chill of the interstellar voids. My brain possesses what no human eye has ever touched.

There is a shot in here of a moon transiting the red eye of Jupiter as the massive gasses swirl in impressionist eddies. I have been here. So often have I stood upon Europa's broken, orange flesh, looking up into the great Jupiter, the looming gasses moving to their impossible rhythms. What it would be to a human eye to see it.

James Irwin: "We lived on another world that was completely 'ours' for three days. It must have been very much like the feelings of Adam and Eve when the Earth was 'theirs.' How to describe it, how to describe it."

An uncanny feeling to lay back and stare up into this massive dome filled with images encircling my body. All of us in this theater lay back and stare up. I cannot escape the idea that this feels like worship.

No one knows what the great majority of the universe consists of. Science states that the everyday matter—the stuff of kitty cats and flowers, our sun, the planets, and the two trillion or so galaxies we can observe—accounts for some 5 percent of being. Dark matter, which may be ordinary matter that is simply invisible to us, or else is matter of an altogether different character than any human has ever imagined, would be approximately 27 percent more. That leaves the mysterious dark energy, even more obscure than dark matter, something of which we know so little that all we can say is that it must be there, otherwise everything cosmology has ever said is false. This accounts for 70 percent of existence.

Our knowledge is still so young. Something fundamental about reality eludes us. We are just a single eyeball catching stray light and making guesses atop guesses. So miraculous the majestic ideas we have managed to claim from our one minuscule point, all in less than a breath of time.

Our planet begins as a ball of heat and rage. Comets and asteroids fill it with water, there is rain for eons, a crust cools atop glowing magma, an ocean covers all. It is believed that during this time there were numerous impacts of objects as wide as 300 miles, which would have sterilized the planet whole and vaporized this world ocean. The waters would have risen into the upper atmosphere, then gradually made their way back down to the surface in the form of slowly descending clouds, thousand-year rains.

Malick visualizes these processes with shots of our present-day Earth. From within cinema's stupor I am convinced they are images of creation.

And then an occurrence that, for all we know, is unique. For billions of years the universe has existed as purely physical forces playing out in a void, but now a certain series of events reaches a result like no other. Instead of moving according to the universe's necessity, matter now begins to want its own logic. An incomprehensibly slow and labyrinthine process. From simple compounds come complex molecules that will populate the Earth.

Riccardo Manzotti: "Why doesn't our behavior simply happen, taking its course the way the planets follow their orbits? We don't know. Just as cosmologists don't know what dark matter is. All we know is that there is something that doesn't add up and very likely points to some profound error in our assumptions about reality."

So comes life into the world. Malick asks: "When did death arrive?"

It has been proposed that the simplest possible definition of life is that which reduces entropy. Any purely physical system moves toward chaos, but life's motive is to create order. This is our novel contribution to the universe. Somehow life discovered a purpose opposite the deepest dictates of being. It strives to sustain this refusal. It fails. Death is the return of entropy.

John Berger: "The concept of entropy is the figure of Death translated into scientific principle."

We are pinned beneath the weight of the global ocean, a fantasia of aquatic creatures writhing and gyring, plumping and pumping. Hundreds of gossamer jellyfish pulsing with neon and passing the waters through their bodies. Life so incubates for billions of years. Then a reckoning for all time: THE FIRST EYE.

Schopenhauer: "The world as representation, with which alone we are dealing with here, certainly begins only with the opening of the first eye."

The world can regard itself. Matter is now perceptions and cognitions, a universe in a mind, an observed world of knowledge but not truth. Estrangement.

Now the enormous lizards that ruled our planet for almost two-hundred million years. Malick takes poetic license into bathos, he attributes to small, bipedal dinosaurs the first complex emotions: compassion, belief, understanding, beauty. Foremost of all: love.

There is a shot of a human-sized dinosaur standing on an idyllic beach before a blissful sunset of ambers, golds, blues. Its reptile eyes stare into the falling sun with wonder. Malick's baffling fancy for dinosaurs is pure indulgence. No scientist of any regard has ever believed that dinosaurs even remotely approached chimpanzee sapience. And perhaps this is why they ruled so long. Our own branch, the primates, has only *existed* for some 60 million years, and our period of dominion is at most 1,000 years. Perhaps the dinosaurs' far superior hegemony explain their appeal to the human imagination. An obsessed child, I commanded the names and details of dozens. The reasons for their disappearance were at that time not theorized, and the children's books I grew up with imparted a great mystery. I remember the final page of a pop-up book, a triceratops fated to extinction, some redness in the western sky, my small head filled with the sense of a plagued world winding down. Was this my first taste of the cycles of iron and gold that gird our understanding? The dinosaur apocalypse has always been to me a special apocalypse, the one I grew up with, the iconic, cinematic apocalypse whose breathtaking grandeur is often made into moving image, the one that feels far more real than all other prophesies. In childhood I naturally inclined toward doomsday. I re-read again and again a encyclopedia entry for Ragnarök. Merely the title of the Book of Revelations chilled me. I read novels about global pandemics, asteroid impacts, malign alien intelligences. I read a scientific book hypothesizing a dim star named Nemesis that hides in the extremities of our solar system and which might one day decimate life on Earth. There was even the haunting last line of Arthur C. Clarke's "The Nine Billion Names of God," where Tibetan monks complete their centuries-long task of writing out all God's names, and the stars begin to quietly extinguish themselves.

The theory of an asteroid impact was introduced in 1980, when I was 2 years old, but it required years to become commonly known and accepted. I still recall the day in the 6th grade when these facts were revealed by our teacher, a kind, fatherly man who did much to spur my intellect. The collision's crater was so large as to only be visible from space; civilizations had lived atop it for thousands of years, but only did we see it once we had learned to escape the Earth's gravity. As our teacher explained the dinosaurs' end I felt initiated into a story of epic scope, a decisive episode from our own *Illiad* detailing the decline of the gods, the death of the heroes, the emergence of we humans.

How many times have I since glimpsed this massive impact? When Malick shows the asteroid burn through the atmosphere, again that uncanny pleasure, to feel as real a thing I have countlessly envisioned by night. The low sound of it tearing through the air, the sight of the dread rock igniting in the sky; on the horizon a detonation and flash unlike any known by human eyes. A sickening second of connection to deep space. My legs grow heavy.

Now the primates, now humans. I once read Jane Goodall because I wanted to know what it was to live among chimpanzees. What I found was human society shorn of all its pretence and mystery, an x-ray to the bone beneath our culture. The chimpanzees greet with hugs, it is a ritual of establishing bonds, maintaining alliances, stifling conflict; now when I hug, I see its animal purpose. I feel some faint awareness of our deep past.

Barthes: "Born of literature, able to speak only with the help of its worn codes, yet I am alone with my strength, doomed *to my own philosophy*."

Humanity looks into a pool of placid water. What was this first moment when a brain fatted with cooked foods grew dense enough to feel its own identity? How did the emergence of this feedback loop change all of existence? Matter now knows that it is matter trapped inside of matter. Death, soul, god, good, evil; they can all now be thought, never explained.

The modern megacity. Soaring cameras stare down at incandescent skyscrapers and funneling lights. The impact of *Koyaanisqatsi* is absolutely clear. All of Malick's originality cannot escape its shadow. Even the music of this sequence is blatantly taken from Philip Glass.

The sun fulfills its destiny, the Earth burns. A verdict of science, whose system of knowledge is complete enough to say what occurred in the first instant after creation and what will be its end. These revelations have been verified with the most rigorous tests devisable. Whether examining the smallest known particles or the faint radiation that has filled the heavens throughout the universe's 14 billion years, these stories have proven correct. Science's claim to secular authority is unimpeachable. The work of one century, our triumph to match the pyramids and cathedrals. And now we are the subjects of this massive labor: entropy will win, the Earth will perish, the universe will unwind.

These points are inarguable, but in the smaller frames we find our will. Nobody knows what countries I might visit next year, what I will eat tomorrow for dinner, how my life will thrive or perish. No one can say what civilization will look like in as little as 50 years, how this one city I inhabit will have changed. We are matter, entropy will claim us, but in the years we hold entropy at bay, we refute science's destiny.

Beckett: "Sleep now, as under that ancient lamp, all twined together, tired out with so much talking, so much listening, so much toil and play."

Now a massive black hole in deep space. The stars are cooling, the universe grows wider and colder, Charybdis swallows all.

At last a blank place, eternities between each lonely drop. No room for anything human; no life, no heat, no radiance, nothing but the crushing grip. A vicious awe to know that this world, me, myself, us, all I've treasured, all I've loved, the wonder that dazzles this mind, all will be broken to the most primeval bits and scattered incoherently.

Now plain dull white. This dome that brought an altered consciousness is again inert. The theater lights grow luminous. From behind, loud jokes about Terrence Malick's hair. I take a deep breath and am not quite so struck by the terror of eternity. Cinema's trance shatters so quickly. The drive home will be dull and trafficky, and twice as long as this fantasia.

Were we members of another era we would be forced to watch this spectacle weekly, our lives always chased by what we saw there. Not this for us. *Voyage of Time* will become just one chit in a hurricane of information.

Except now I have written about it. So, for me it will not. That is one purpose of these essays, to dwell within these fourteen films that have asserted their need to be remembered. Now I will *never* forget them.

Science is of human design, a form of comprehension as fatally flawed as all human comprehension; it is not a godhead, not a verity, not a gleaming ocean liner come to snatch us out these deeps. Its grip on our comprehension will one day loosen. A child of its world, I take its lessons, ever mindful that when I stare into the stars they are the same lights that have lodged my species' dreams since our very first eyes stared skyward.

Mary Ruefle: "To reread a book is to make a pollard of it."

A pollard is a tree whose branches have been trimmed so that they might grow back to range more widely. In watching Malick's journey through being I have made a pollard of that mystery Stephen Hawking gave me exactly 20 years prior, the mystery that prompted Errol Morris to film Hawking's thoughts about the beginning of time and its ultimate fate. And now Malick has given me the perspective from which to reflect that in those twenty years I have repeatedly made a pollard of what that film gave me. Again and again I have chopped back that mystery, and so it has grown like kudzu, sprouting more mysteries for me to make more pollards of.

What is this tree of thought that grows into the thoughts that will prune it and will also feed it? Where in this limitless growth does one mystery end and the next mystery begin? It is from this savage forest that I am making the space for myself. I am fashioning my own perceptions. These are the words that double reality.

OFFICIAL
CCM ◑

GET OUT OF JAIL
* VOUCHER *

- -

Tear this out.

Skip that social event.

It's okay.

You don't have to go if you don't want to. Pick up
the book you just bought. Open to the first page.
You'll thank us by the third paragraph.

If friends ask why you were a no-show, show them
this voucher.

You'll be fine.

- -

We're coping.

◑

CPSIA information can be obtained
at www.ICGtesting.com
Printed in the USA
LVOW12s1606180917
549132LV00003B/579/P